THIRD GRADE SURVIVAL GUIDE

Fun Tips, Exam Strategies, & More To Rock 3rd Grade!

Bobbie Anderson Jr

Copyright 2025 by Bobbie Anderson Jr.
- ALL Rights Reserved

In no way is it legal to reproduce, duplicate, or transmit any part of this document in either electronic means or in printed format. Recording of this publication is strictly prohibited and any storage of this document is not allowed unless with written permission from the publisher.

Thank you for buying our book and supporting our mission to provide accessible resources for everyone!

Instructions for Word Search Puzzles

- Hidden words are key vocabulary of each chapter
- Some words are combined. For example, "third grade" is hidden as "thirdgrade".
- Words are hidden in forward, horizontal, vertical, in reverse, and four diagonal directions (top-left, top-right, bottom-left, bottom-right).
- STUCK? The parenthesis shows combined words.

To avoid any potential bleed-through while solving word search puzzles with certain pens or markers, simply place a blank sheet of thicker paper behind the page you're working on.

↑   ↑

This guide is more than just a book—it's a comprehensive third-grade study resource designed to address every aspect of a student's journey. Whether your child is mastering math, navigating group projects, or preparing for exams, the Third Grade Survival Guide will help your child rock third grade like a ROCKSTAR!

Each chapter ends with a fun word search puzzle that reinforces key concepts, making learning enjoyable and helping kids retain knowledge effectively.

Table of Contents

Chapter 1: The Big Day: Conquering the First Day of Third Grade 7

Chapter 2: How to Pick the Right Friends in Third Grade 15

Chapter 3: How to Handle Disagreements in the
Third-Grade Classroom 23

Chapter 4: How to Handle Disagreements on the Playground 31

Chapter 5: Asking the Right Questions in Third Grade 39

Chapter 6: How to Be a Great Team Player in Small Groups 47

Chapter 7: How to Succeed in Studying Third Grade History 55

Chapter 8: How to Succeed in Studying Third Grade Math 63

Chapter 9: How to Become a Reading Rockstar in Third Grade 71

Chapter 10: How to Crush It in Third Grade P.E. 79

Chapter 11: How to Be a Science Superstar in Third Grade 89

Chapter 12: How to Rock Third Grade Writing 97

Chapter 13: How to Conquer Third Grade Homework 107

Chapter 14: How to Be an Exam-Ready Rockstar in Third Grade 117

Word Search Solutions .... 127 - 141

BELONGS TO

■■

CHAPTER 1

The Big Day: Conquering the First Day of Third Grade

Hey there, newbie, the first day of third grade is just around the corner. It's totally normal to feel a little nervous, super excited, or even both. This book will help you handle it like a pro. Let's get started. Here are some things to know to make your first day amazing.

1. Rise & Shine

First things first. Having a morning routine is a wonderful way to start your day. Your morning routine begins the night before by setting your alarm. This way, you're not rushing around in the morning because you overslept. Eat a nutritious breakfast, like scrambled eggs, toast, or even a bowl of your favorite cereal. Fuel up so your brain is ready to work.

Pro tip: Lay out your clothes the night before. This way, you're not losing time in the morning wondering if polka dot and striped clothing matches (spoiler alert: they don't).

2. Walking Through the Doors

When you get to school, you'll probably see familiar and unfamiliar faces. Your teacher will be at the door with a big smile, welcoming everyone. Here's your first job: smile back and say, "Hi!" It's simple, but it sets a positive tone for the day.

Where's my seat? Don't sweat it, most teachers will have name tags on desks to help you out. If unsure; just ask! Teachers love helping new students get settled.

3. Icebreakers: Get Ready to Mix & Mingle

A surefire way to get everyone talking is an icebreaker. This activity is a fun way for everyone to share something about themselves. You might play a game like "Two Truths and a Lie," where you share two true things about yourself and one that's false.

For example:
1. I went to Disneyland during summer break.
2. I can speak three languages.
3. My pet hamster is named Cheeto.
Can you guess which one's the lie?

Pro tip: Keep in mind that this is the first day for everyone. So, you won't be the only one feeling nervous or shy.

4. Surprises & Supplies

Do you like surprises? Usually, teachers leave little welcome gifts on desks, like a pencil with a fun eraser or a bookmark. It's their way of saying, "Welcome to the team!"
Your teacher will spend time explaining how supplies will be used for the year. Most likely, your teacher will have special organizers for storing your pencils, crayons, notebooks, and folders. Keeping your supplies organized helps your workday flow better.

5. Rules & Routines

Every classroom has rules.Don't worry; they're not there to ruin your fun. Your teacher will go over the rules for the classroom and how these rules will keep things running smoothly throughout the year. What if your teacher lets you help create the rules? How cool is that?

You might already know some of the basic classroom rules, such as:
- Raise your hand to speak.
- Be kind to classmates.
- Line up quietly in the line.

You'll also learn routines, like how to line up, where to put completed homework, and what signals to use if you need to use the bathroom.

Pro tip: Pay close attention to these routines. Knowing them makes you a pro.

6. Lunchtime Adventures

Lunchtime is a big part of your day. You'll finally get to relax and see what's packed in your lunchbox or grab a tray from the cafeteria. Where do I sit? Usually, you'll sit with classmates. Look for kids who were in your icebreaker group earlier or someone sitting alone and ask, "May I join you?" They'll probably be super glad you did—instant connection!

Pro Tip: If you're nervous about opening your milk carton or peeling an orange, ask a lunch aide or teacher. They're there for you.

7. Recess: Fun time!

Recess is your time. Whether you're into swinging, playing kickball, or just chatting with friends, this is your chance to have fun and blow off steam. If you're not sure what to do, try joining a game that has already started. Just say, "May I play?" Most kids will say yes.

8. What If Things Go Wrong?

Let's be real: something may go wrong. Maybe you spill your water bottle, trip on the way to class, or forget someone's name. Guess what? That's okay! Nobody's perfect, and everyone makes mistakes. If something embarrassing happens, laugh it off. Learning to roll with the punches is a great way to de-escalate embarrassing situations.

9. Wrapping Up the Day

Before you know it, the day will be over. Your teacher might give you a quick preview of tomorrow's activities. You might be given a fun homework assignment, like drawing a picture or writing about your favorite summer memory.
When the bell rings, take a deep breath. You made it! You completed your first day of third grade. High five yourself. No, seriously, do it.

10. A Few Bonuses:

- **Stay curious:** If you don't know something, ask! Don't be afraid to ask questions. Your questions will help others learn too.
- **Be friendly:** A smile and a kind word go a long way.
- **Go easy on yourself.** It's okay to struggle when learning new things. Struggling shows that you're just missing some information. Ask questions to get the needed information to make it easier to understand. Remember—you're learning something new, and it'll get easier.

So, there you have it! With these tips in your back pocket, you're ready to conquer the first day of third grade like a champ. You've got this!

Chapter 1 The Big Day: Conquering the First Day of Third Grade

```
V F R S Q R M F S E I L P P U S W H X H J V J
L J T X E J N A P X W I Q Z M I P Y V K Q R W
I L V C S B V Y C U R I O U S M M I B L F H B
M Z E P U B Q O L F U D E R Y A C B U L K V G
G S G U B T T N L D I E K J S F M P R A C F A
S Q V M M Z U C R P N K H O O Y X M E U D A C
J S V U Y Z Y X W B H E U L W Z R A C G R D Y
A B S A F N S C W R V P I K I E C P Z H U P O
W L M Z D N F Q O P F X A R K C R L F J S O E
K T S I Q U Y N W J G K M A F Q Y P K U N K C
P G F R S D H A D O W L E A U T Z T U Q N S Q
T H X E I D R L C T I R Z C K P L R L P A M L
H P L I K U O F G L B T E V U E H R C H R I R
I U I T H G V I B E J F G E N I T U O R P L H
R K Q F N B K G C O I N D S Z M G T J Y X E B
D P L A D J L I W R G E N L U N C H T I M E V
G G G T W Y Z B S Q C N Q K O A A Q I P C G R
R S Z T R G I T P X R W E U V F K Y L D L T V
A U U B E C D N I R H Q G H C Q F X G M A V T
D A A Q B A M W O H N F B R W A F B O W K U J
E G J U Y L O M F W P W H Q X L F O N U V O S
G T E I Z U F Y P I E O X U T X U T Z U O M R
D D P V I A C O N Q U E R D E N V P T D X Q F
```

conquer
curious
firstday (first day)
friendly
icebreaker

laugh
lunchtime
recess
routine
rules

smile
supplies
thirdgrade (third grade)

CHAPTER 2

How to Pick the Right Friends in Third Grade

Making friends in third grade can be a big deal! Some friends might like the same games, shows, or snacks as you. Others might be completely different but still make awesome friends. The trick is learning how to pick the right friends who make you happy, help you grow, and have fun with you. Here are some ideas and real-life examples to help you choose the right crew.

1. Look for Kindness First

The most important thing in a friend is kindness. Pay attention to how people treat you and others. Do they smile and help when someone drops their books? Do they say kind words to others? Do they take turns during games? These are clues that someone could be a great friend.

Real-Life Scenario:
Let's say you're on the playground and you trip during a game of tag. A kid named Cindy stops, helps you up, and asks if you're okay. That's a sign that Cindy might be a good friend because she's caring.

2. Find Someone Who Likes the Same Things

Friends who share your interests make life more fun! If you love soccer, look for kids who also enjoy kicking the ball around at recess. If you're into drawing, see who's doodling during free time. Having something in common makes it easier to connect.

Real-Life Scenario:
During art class, you notice a boy named Evan drawing a superhero that you like. You start talking about superheroes, and before you know it, you're brainstorming your own comic strip together. Boom! Friendship!

3. Watch for Good Listening Skills

A great friend listens to you and cares about what you say. If someone is always interrupting or talking only about themselves, they might not be the best fit. Good friends take turns talking and asking questions like, "What did you do this weekend?" or "How are you feeling?"

Real-Life Scenario:
You tell your table partner, Helen, about your new puppy. Instead of changing the subject, she smiles and asks, "What's his name?". That's how you know Helen is interested and could be a great friend.

4. Pay Attention to How They Make You Feel
Do you feel happy and comfortable when you're with someone? That's a good sign! If someone makes you feel bad about yourself, left out, or worried might not be the right friend for you.

Real-Life Scenario:
You sit next to Ariana at lunch, and she keeps teasing you about your favorite backpack. You feel sad every time you're around her. On the other hand, Blake always laughs at your jokes and makes you feel like a superstar. Stick with Blake.

5. Look for People Who Are Honest

Honesty is super important in a friendship. You want friends who tell the truth and don't spread rumors. If someone says, "I promise I'll save you a seat," and they do it, that's a good sign.

Real-Life Scenario:
One day, your friend Max tells you he forgot his homework, but later you find out he just didn't do it. Another friend, Sophia, admits when she makes mistakes and always keeps her promises. Who sounds like a better friend?

6. Be Open to New People

Sometimes best friends are the ones you don't expect. Maybe the new kid in class is shy, but once you talk to him, you find out he loves the same video game as you. Maybe, someone who's not in your class invites you to play a game, at recess, you've never tried before.

Real-Life Scenario:
You're sitting alone during indoor recess, and Ava, who you don't know well, asks if you want to play Uno. You join her game and realize she's super funny. Now you've made a new friend!

7. Don't Be Afraid to Move On

Sometimes friendships don't work out, and that's okay. Maybe someone isn't kind or starts ignoring you. Move on! It's best to spend time with people who treat you well.
Real-Life Scenario:
Your friend Jake keeps leaving you out during group projects and whispering with other kids. It hurts your feelings, so you decide to hang out with Sam instead. Sam always invites you to join and makes you feel included. Who's the better buddy?

8. Be a Good Friend Yourself

Friendship is a two-way street. To make great friends, you need to be a great friend too. That means being kind, honest, and fun to be around. Help someone who's struggling and listen when your friends talk. Treat others the way you want them to treat you.

Real-Life Scenario:
One day, your friend Kayla forgets her lunch. You share your sandwich with her, and she smiles and says, "You're the best!" Being thoughtful like this helps you keep your friendships strong.

9. Don't Worry About Having a Million Friends

It's better to have one or two amazing friends than a whole bunch of friends who aren't nice to you. Quality over quantity always works!

Real-Life Scenario:
Your classmate Liam has tons of friends but always seems upset because some of them are mean to him. Your crew might be smaller, but everyone in it treats each other with respect. Quantity in friendship is overrated!

10. Practice Patience

Sometimes it takes time to find the right friends. Don't rush it! Keep being yourself and kind to others, and soon enough, you'll meet them.

Real-Life Scenario:
First, you feel like no one in your class likes the same things as you. Then, a month later, you join the school's Lego club and meet Harper, who's just as obsessed with building castles as you are. Friendship success!

Remember, best friends are the ones who make you feel happy, safe, and excited to come to school every day. Trust your gut, be kind, and have fun making new friends!

Chapter 2 How to Pick the Right Friends in Third Grade

```
G R D I G B A C Q L P S Y X D Y F H A E S V L
G Z Y T I L A U Q Y R D L D T F I N Z B J J Z
Z A O U P X T L G N G R M T W D F U U B I M G
Z Y K M E T S L U D R B V W U Z W F V C T Y E
R X R O P C E T I F D R B B R N O M L L H F M
R N L V W U N Q E B T Y M H D Q T M Y R X E C
H D N E I F O Y X F A H E B L L G Q X P Z H O
S F J O P T H Y B W A P G O Z K G Q Y R P Y N
T D X N P K I N D N E S S U L E U O H N I A A
R I N E U C V A H A X X L Q O H V M J Q H B H
D X S E T D Y S A J V N L R A H Q X E L S D A
N W H E I I N X X K E T O Z T H T E U C D B M
V P U C G R L B O B N Y Z I P Z Q W V M N N C
F T H K R B F C J P X J G Y P M B L A H E X V
M Y N M D G T W F I Q I U W Q N T Y H V I O J
X R F L D B V B E L E P P D D W C Y K U R X V
C I G F U G X U S X B B M W P D O Q M G F C J
F G Z L H I R A O M E F U N H N L H X X O L C
F H L U W H M Z G O C V D B D H P F W M J R J
J T R B O P Y F T E E L B A T R O F M O C M Z
W C C Z S Q C Q M F N E T S I L I O V P A U C
I Y C O K E S Q K K Y U C C I R N B H Q O C Y
V Y F F H H C K I V V T F L Y B F P U O M R R
```

comfortable   honest   right
common   kindness   safe
friends   listen   thoughtful
friendship   moveon (move on)
happy   quality

CHAPTER 3

How to Handle Disagreements in the Third-Grade Classroom

Disagreements happen. That's just part of being human. Even best friends don't agree on everything all the time. So, what do you do when someone in your class sees things differently than you do? Don't worry, it's not the end of the world! In fact, learning how to handle disagreements can help you become an awesome problem solver and an even better friend. Here are some ways to deal with tricky situations you might run into.

1. Stay Calm (Even When You're Angry)

Real-Life Scenario:
You and your classmate, Chris, are working on a group project. You want to build a spaceship for your diorama, but Chris insists on building a castle. Suddenly, you're arguing, and it feels like a tug-of-war with words.

What should you do?

First, take a deep breath. It's challenging to solve a problem when you're upset. Count to ten or take a sip of water if you need to cool down. Staying calm helps you think clearly, and it shows that you're serious about fixing the problem, not just fighting about it.
Try this: Say, "Let's take a minute to think before we decide." This gives everyone a chance to relax and reset.

2. Listen First

Sometimes, disagreements happen because no one's really listening. Have you ever been so busy trying to explain your side that you didn't hear what the other person was saying? It's like trying to play a video game without turning on the screen—you're missing the entire picture!

Let's go back to the spaceship vs. castle debate. Ask Chris why he wants to build a castle. Maybe he has a cool idea, like adding a working drawbridge. Listening to his idea doesn't mean you're giving up on yours; it shows you respect his opinion.

Try this: Say, "Why do you think a castle would be better? I want to hear your idea." Then, really listen to Chris without interrupting.

3. Use "I" Statements

When you're in disagreement, it's easy to blame the other person. But saying things like "You're wrong" or "You're not listening" can make the other person feel attacked. Instead, utilize "I" statements to express your emotions without assigning blame.

For example, say, "I feel frustrated because I really wanted to do a spaceship." This tells Chris how you're feeling without making him feel like he's in trouble.

Try this: Practice turning "You" statements into "I" statements. Instead of saying, "You're being bossy," try saying, "I feel like my ideas aren't being heard."

4. Look for a Compromise

A compromise is like a win-win solution where both people get a little of what they want. Maybe Chris really wants a castle, and you really want a spaceship. What if you build a castle with a rocket launcher attached? Suddenly, you've got a super-cool combo that makes both of you happy.

Real-Life Scenario:
Your friend Emma wants to play tag at recess, but you want to play kickball. Instead of arguing, you could say, "How about we play tag first and then kickball after?" Finding middle ground shows that you care about both others' ideas.

5. Ask a Teacher for Help (When You Need It)

Sometimes, no matter how hard you try, you just can't agree. That's okay! Asking a teacher or another adult for help isn't tattling. It's being responsible when you can't solve a problem on your own.

Real-Life Scenario:
You and Mia both want to be the line leader, but neither of you will back down. Instead of fighting over it, you can say, "Mrs. Carson, can you help us figure this out?" Teachers are excellent at helping you find fair solutions.

6. Practice Forgiveness

Let's imagine that you and your friend Alex had a disagreement about who should take turns on the swings. As the argument escalated, Alex uttered some hurtful words. Later, Alex apologizes. What should you do? Forgive him! Holding a grudge only makes you feel worse. Accept their apology and move on. Forgiveness helps you both feel better and keeps your friendship strong.

Try this: Say, "It's cool. I know we were both upset. Let's be friends."

7. Learn from the Situation

Every disagreement is a chance to learn something new. Maybe you'll discover how to compromise better, how to stand up for yourself, or how to listen more carefully. The next time you have a disagreement, you'll be even better at handling it.

Real-Life Scenario:
Last time you argued with a classmate, you got upset and stormed off. This time, you remembered to stay calm and talk it out. That's progress!

Quick Tips to Remember

- Take deep breaths when you feel upset.
- Listen to the other person's side without interrupting.
- Use "I" statements to share your feelings.
- Look for ways to compromise so both people feel happy.
- Ask for help if the disagreement gets too big to handle on your own.
- Forgive and move on when it's over.
- Learn from every disagreement so you're ready for the next one.

Final Thought

Disagreements don't have to ruin your day. They're just a part of life, like homework or lunchtime spills. If handled properly, they can make you stronger and smarter. Therefore, the next time you and a classmate disagree, remember to remain composed, actively listen, and resolve the issue like the capable third grader you are!

Chapter 3 How to Handle Disagreements in the Third Grade Classroom

```
I D J N R V Y R Y O H I D B C F B T G K S I Z
T N H E E J I U U C S D I N Q W N H Q P X N G
J K L N W Y N E O T C W F B E J C R R U B X F
Z A L F E B S M A W A D S O E V A W F D Q O M
X Z U L N Q P T D I S A G R E E M E N T G R Z
V O E E V R E E P G J U J U W G G L S H W F G
M P P P O M D D S B J T N R J Q C H V P H H W
M U W M E Z I P B L X E G R F L L D Y D J Z T
S F I N F I F H N E Y Y V M R A Q F U R H M Z
D S T F O R G I V E N E S S H E N T Z O U I C
E S P U T D R U H X W K E Z Q T S N L L Q C L
Z E M O T I O N M T W X H M Y K Q P L G R Y U
U V K Y A H W G V W P C Y M L U Q W E N Q L F
B R Q R O O C I N R G X B E W A I Z Y C L H M
D O T P W B O G E H I L G L M G C R P A T E M
J M G Q B M P S H M U L S B I O N Y C W K L C
F Q G T J Y S O H U P Q J O C O O H A P V P P
D M B Z A S C Z V Q I C Q R X C I E D T Y C J
E Y U H J O D Z I A C F E P Z T N W Y M S G N
Q S X B X T I F F D P T C F J E I O I Y S R P
Q O M U V V F I U R P A C E E W P O P J A R T
M H L W Q L B V P L S N H B O C O X Q E D E J
T W W I O Y Z W S Y Y E M U J T L M L J K A J
```

compromise   help   problem
disagreement   istatements   relax
emotion   (I statements)   respect
express   learn   staycalm (stay calm)
forgiveness   opinion

CHAPTER 4

How to Handle Disagreements on the Playground

The playground is one of the best parts of third grade. It's where you get to run, play, and have fun with your friends. However, unexpected events can occur. Maybe someone cuts in line at the slide, or two kids can't agree on the rules of a game. Disagreements happen, but guess what? That's totally normal! The positive news is, there are ways to handle these situations so everyone can get back to having fun.

Here are some ideas and real-life examples to help you handle disagreements on the playground like a pro:

1. Use Your Words
When something goes wrong, the first step is to talk about it. It can feel tempting to yell or stomp away, but calmly saying what's bothering you works much better.

Real-Life Scenario:
You're playing tag, and another kid tags you when you're standing on the "safe" spot. Instead of shouting, "That's not fair!" you could say, "Hey, I thought I was on base. Can we talk about the rules so it's fair for everyone?" Using kind and clear words helps the other person understand your point of view.

2. Take Turns and Share

Sometimes disagreements arise when everyone wants the same thing. Sharing and taking turns is a simple way to fix this.

Real-Life Scenario:
Let's say your class gets new playground equipment, and everyone wants to use the swings. Instead of arguing, you can suggest a timer system: "How about we each get five minutes and then switch?" Taking turns makes sure everyone gets a chance to have fun.

3. Play Rock, Paper, Scissors

Believe it or not, this little game can solve a lot of problems! If you can't agree on who goes first or which game to play, a quick round of rock, paper, scissors can decide for you. It's fast, fair, and keeps things moving.

Real-Life Scenario:
You and a friend both want to be the seeker in hide-and-seek. Instead of arguing, play one round of rock, paper, scissors. The winner gets to go first, and the other person gets their turn next.

4. Ask a Grown-Up for Help
Sometimes, a disagreement gets too big to handle on your own. If no one can agree or feelings are getting hurt, it's okay to ask a teacher or playground supervisor to step in.

Real-Life Scenario:
You're playing soccer, and a few kids start arguing over whether a goal counts. The game is stopping, and everyone's getting frustrated. You can say, "Let's ask the teacher to help us figure it out so we can keep playing." Grown-ups are there to help solve problems, not to get anyone in trouble.

5. Walk Away if Things Get Too Heated

If someone is yelling or refusing to listen, it might be time to step back. Walking away doesn't mean you're giving up; it means you're staying calm and letting everyone cool off.

Real-Life Scenario:
You're playing basketball, and another player keeps insisting they're right about a rule, even though you know it's not true. Instead of arguing, you can say, "Let's take a break and figure this out later." Then, go play something else for a while.

6. Try to See the Other Person's Point of View

Sometimes, disagreements happen because we don't understand how someone else is feeling. Taking a moment to think about their perspective can help.

Real-Life Scenario:
You're playing four square, and someone gets mad when they're out. Instead of saying, "Stop being a sore loser," you could say, "I know it's frustrating to get out. Do you want to talk about it?" Showing kindness can turn the situation around.

7. Make a Compromise

A compromise means everyone gives a little to solve the problem. It may not be perfect, but it's better than arguing and not having fun.
Real-Life Scenario:
You and a friend want to play different games. Instead of fighting over it, you could say, "Let's play your game first and mine after." That way, both of you win.

8. Apologize if You Need To

If you realize you've done something wrong, saying "I'm sorry" can make a huge difference. It's not always easy, but it shows you care about making things right.
Real-Life Scenario:
You're playing tag and accidentally push someone too hard when tagging them. You can say, "I'm sorry for pushing you. I didn't mean to. Are you okay?" A little apology can go a long way.

9. Stick to the Rules

Many playground arguments happen because people aren't clear on the rules of a game. Before starting, take a few minutes to agree on the rules so everyone is on the same page.

Real-Life Scenario:
Before starting kickball, you can say, "Let's all agree on how many outs we get and whether we're playing with stealing bases." Clear rules = fewer arguments.

10. Know When to Let It Go

Sometimes, the best way to handle a disagreement is to move on. Not every problem needs to be solved right away. If the argument isn't a big deal, it's okay to say, "Let's just play something else."

Real-Life Scenario:
You're engaged in a heated argument with a friend about who made the first touch on home base in a game of tag. Instead of going back and forth forever, you could say, "It's not worth it. Let's just start a new game."

Final Thoughts

Disagreements on the playground happen to everyone, but they don't have to ruin your fun. By using your words, staying calm, and working together to solve problems, you can keep the playground a happy place for everyone. Remember, being a loyal friend means listening, sharing, and trying your best to get along. And if things get tough, there's always another recess tomorrow!

Chapter 4 How to Handle Disagreements on the Playground

```
W N D U K P G D M A E W Z H M Z P R O U M P R
K N W N H A H Q M U D T U L M M P Y G Y K K K
K B F D R P H P Y A W A K L A W N W L U Q R G
J D D E O E O G Q V N N I N A Y G Z G V N Y B
U C B R S R W I C H R V B V D V H O L J N J Y
D M S S I V U C L A O D L O M G H L L Q J A K
U C F T V Z B P W M Z K U L H H Z R T M T I C
S B X A R Y E T F R B I F K Q C I E Q M L K O
V R Y N E C L G Z Y S I E V I T C E P S R E P
A A E D P H M W U N I S M L V H J L Q O C Q B
Y J Y C U X A Q R G Q R P H B W A Y G H P V X
S B P X S A K U T L K I F Q I Y U Y I P W P Z
G B K K J V T H Q M F D V Y G G X I L V Q A P
Q Z Q E F G F X H W Q W D R S L M P R L S Y F
B V I O N A Y G S T O G O A O A X B O G C J T
U B P I L F S P E D H U B Q P N J I C Q I B N
T X K O T H I Q U V N N X D P O D L K Z S T F
X A Q R A I G R G D Y N X R F M L L T C S O G
T A G R J B I A B R Y T O R T A S O I Z O U Q
D O I W R E S F L J T B L V Q B V J G N R K J
I N J V L Y U Q M E L R Y G H N H R H I S E C
G M T C Y H Z V U E Y S Q I J Z Q L E O Z D Q
I S U B O I H T M P Q M W M K E S O L V E E J
```

apologize	rock	takingturns
paper	scissors	(taking turns)
perspective	sharing	understand
playground	solve	walkaway
problem	supervisor	

CHAPTER 5

Asking the Right Questions in Third Grade

Asking questions unlocks a wealth of information. In third grade, you're learning so many new things, and the best way to make sure you understand everything is to ask good questions. But what does it mean to ask the right questions? Don't worry. These real-life examples and fun tips will help you become a question-asking expert!

Why Ask Questions?

Think of questions like keys that unlock answers. When you ask questions, you're showing your teacher, classmates, and even yourself that you're curious and ready to learn. Plus, asking questions helps you when:

- You're stuck on a math problem.
- You're unsure about what your teacher just explained.
- You're working on a group project and need everyone to understand the plan.
- You're curious about something cool your classmate mentioned.

Asking questions isn't just for when you're confused. It's also a way to dive deeper and learn even more about something interesting!

When Is the Right Time to Ask a Question?

Timing is important. Here are some real-life third grade scenarios to help you figure out the best time to ask your question:

1. During a lesson:
Raise your hand if your teacher says something you don't understand. For example:
Your teacher is explaining fractions, and you're thinking, "Wait, what does the top number mean?" Raise your hand and ask, "What does the numerator do in a fraction?"

2. After the lesson:
If you're still confused after the lesson ends, go up to your teacher quietly and say, "I didn't quite get it when you talked about numerators; can you explain it again?"

3. In group work:
If your team is building a volcano for a science project and someone says, "Let's use baking soda," but you're not sure how it works, ask, "How does baking soda help the volcano erupt?"

4. Not during quiet time:
If the class is reading silently, save your question for later. Write it down so you won't forget!

How to Ask a Good Question

Not all questions are the same. A good question helps you get the best answer. Here are some ideas for asking great questions:

1. Be specific:
Instead of saying, "I don't get it," try, "Can you explain how to round numbers to the nearest ten?" This tells your teacher exactly what you need help with.

2. Stay on topic:
If your class is learning about animals in science, asking, "What's for lunch?" is not the best choice. Save off-topic questions for later.

3. Ask to learn more:
You can ask questions even when you understand the basics. For example:
The teacher says, "Penguins live in cold places." You can ask, "How do penguins stay warm in icy water?"

4. Use question words:
Start your questions with words like:
- Who (Who invented multiplication?)
- What (What does "déjà vu" mean?)
- Where do monarch butterflies migrate?)
- When (When do we use a thesaurus?
- Why (Why do plants need sunlight?)
- How (How do astronauts eat in space?)

Real-Life Scenarios of Question Power

Here are some real-life examples of how asking questions can make your third-grade experience amazing:

1. Science Class Confusion:
Your teacher shows a video about the water cycle. You see words like "evaporation" and "condensation," but you're confused about what they mean. You raise your hand and ask, "Can you explain how evaporation works?" Your teacher smiles and says, "Great question!" Then she draws a diagram on the board that helps the whole class understand better.

2. Math Magic :
You're learning how to multiply, but the numbers are starting to look like a big jumble. Instead of giving up, you ask, "Can you show me another way to solve this?" Your teacher introduces a fun trick called skip counting, and suddenly, multiplying is way easier!

3. Recess Curiosity:
Your friend says their older sibling told them about "black holes" in space. You're super curious and ask, "What's a black hole?" They explain what they know, but you're still wondering. Back in class, you ask your teacher, "Why do black holes pull everything in?" The teacher promises to find a cool video for the next science lesson.

What If You're Nervous to Ask?

It's okay to feel shy about raising your hand. Here's how to get past that:

1. Remember:
No question is silly. If you don't understand something, chances are other classmates are wondering the same thing.

2. Write it down first:
If you're nervous about saying your question out loud, jot it down. You can ask later when you feel ready.

3. Ask a friend:
If you're unsure about something, ask a classmate before asking the teacher. They might explain it in a way you understand.

4. Start small:
If you're shy, practice asking one question a day. The more you do it, the easier it gets!

Bonus Tips for Question Experts

- Help others: If a classmate is confused but too shy to ask, encourage them to speak up or ask the question for them.
- Be polite: Say, "Excuse me," or "Can I ask a question?" before speaking.
- Practice at home: Ask questions at home about things you see or read. This helps you get better at forming great questions in class.

Final Thought

Asking questions is one of the best ways to learn and grow. In third grade, you're surrounded by teachers, friends, and even books that are ready to help you find answers. So go ahead—raise that hand, open your mouth, and let your curiosity shine. Your next exciting discovery might be just one question away!

Chapter 5 Asking the Right Questions in Third Grade

```
K O L P I C Z G Q I X G H M M H V Y C A T G F
S Q O E A M K U O V M P N Z U C Y D B X Y Q J
A L A N J M N V J F U E M I Z O C R T H L A L
N Z Q V I L C P X R M C Y Y R U L J N L K F V
S Z I V G O U P K C A N V W O T E Z X Z Z B D
N Y J Z D E D Q N I S D Q S U D K W S K W I Z
P S P E C I F I C Y C F A T D G E K N B E R A
C K B G J P Q C T P L A R K Y P J S O X Q O E
Z D N I P N M T I M I N G G X Z V G I W N P C
T S I V Y R V A G A X G E C Y O X K T Q I W Q
W M V Q R L V F D E S C Z U V Z A V S I A I E
B B W K Q S O T W M H N W X D G T A E M L Z C
P O M K O J T L H R H G O Q R V P O U P P G U
H X H G Q S T H E L M W X C U E O D Q O X H R
F M G O B M L E R K N X Z Y X Q I R V R E P I
O S H T S Z B F E H W T H N X H T Q F T L F O
N K H X J N S P W X A W B L P O I F L A L G U
H K N T K N P Q J H K V P T M S V E O N W K S
S D T Y F P D O W P P S R O T V A N L T N O F
B C A M O E V G Q Q X H F N M R C Q Y C A A I
G F Y P H M L S W S M R A F N T C Y M T M H J
N T B S W G B Z N B W I Y E J T X W V P L W C
X J K U K W S J Y X M S C M S I L W W Q S S H
```

ask	learn	where
curious	questions	who
explain	specific	why
how	timing	
important	what	

CHAPTER 6

How to Be a Great Team Player in Small Groups

Working with a small group in your third-grade classroom can be awesome! You get to share ideas, learn from each other, and create something cool together. But it can also be tricky. What if someone doesn't agree with your idea? What if one person wants to do all the work, or worse, none at all? Don't worry, this chapter will teach you how to work with others like a pro and make group work fun and successful.

Why Is Teamwork Important?

Imagine trying to build a giant LEGO tower all by yourself. It might take forever! However, a team can do it faster and more creatively.

Teamwork helps you:

- Solve problems together.
- Learn new ideas from your classmates.
- Get the job done faster and better.
- Build friendships and have fun!

But teamwork doesn't just happen magically. It takes effort, kindness, and practice. Here's how you can be a fantastic team player.

Step 1: Listen Like a Pro

Everyone in a group wants to have their ideas heard. That's why listening is so important. Here's how you can be an awesome listener:

- Look at the person who's talking. It shows you care about what they're saying.
- Don't interrupt. Hold off on sharing your thoughts until they've finished.
- Repeat what they said. Try saying, "So you think we should draw the poster first? That's a cool idea."

Real-Life Scenario:
You're working on a science project about animals. Mia says, "I think we should start by listing the animals that live in the rainforest." Instead of saying, "No, let's draw pictures first," you can say, "That's a wonderful idea, Mia. Maybe we can make the list and then draw the pictures." Boom—teamwork activated!

Step 2: Share Your Ideas (Nicely!)

Don't be afraid to speak up! Your ideas are important, too. But remember, how you share them matters. Here's how to do it:
- Use kind words. Say, "What if we try this?" instead of "My idea is better."
- Be clear. Explain your idea so everyone understands.
- Be flexible. If your team decides to go with another idea, it's okay. You'll have more chances to share.

Real-Life Scenario:
Your group is building a model of a volcano. You think using red paper for lava would look amazing. You say, "What if we use red paper for the lava? It'll make it look more realistic!" Even if the group decides to use paint instead, you've shown you're a terrific team player by sharing your ideas kindly.

Step 3: Solve Problems Together

Sometimes, things don't go smoothly in a group. Maybe two people want to do the same job, or someone doesn't agree with an idea. Here's how to handle it:

- Stay calm. Getting upset won't help.
- Talk it out. Say, "Let's figure this out together."
- Find a compromise. Maybe you can combine two ideas or take turns.

Real-Life Scenario:
You're making a poster for a history project, and both Sam and Taylor want to do the writing. You say, "How about Taylor writes the title and Sam writes the facts? That way, you both get to help." Problem solved!

Step 4: Do Your Part

Every team member has a job to do. If someone doesn't help, it makes things harder for everyone else. Be the kind of teammate who:

- Volunteers for tasks. Don't wait for someone else to do it.
- Finishes what you start. If you promised to glue pictures, keep your promise to glue the pictures on the poster.
- Encourages others. Say "You're doing great!" to keep everyone motivated.

Real-Life Scenario:
Your group is making a diorama of a pioneer village. Your job is to make tiny houses. Even if it's tricky, you keep going and finish your part, so the group's project is complete. Everyone will appreciate your hard work!

Step 5: Celebrate Success

When your group finishes a project, take a moment to celebrate! Say things like:

- "We did an awesome job!"
- "Thanks for working so hard, everyone."
- "I'm proud of what we made together."

Celebrating shows you value everyone's effort, and it makes teamwork even more fun.

Quick Tips for Teamwork

- If someone is shy, ask for their opinion. Say, "What do you think we should do, Emma?"
- If someone is bossy, remind them nicely that everyone gets a turn to share ideas.
- If your group gets stuck, ask your teacher for help. That's what they're there for!

Final Thoughts

Working in a small group can feel like an adventure. Sometimes it's challenging, but if you listen, share, solve problems, and do your part, you'll be an amazing teammate. And who knows? You might even make some new friends along the way.

So, the next time your teacher says, "Get into groups," don't worry. You've got this! Go be the team player everyone wants on their side.

Chapter 6 How to Be a Great Team Player in Small Groups

```
C R X O Z B J O H S T B S M A L L S S U X J P
I E Q C Z C E B R H S O U K O U C O D U F O C
Y G G G X U M R P A I N G N K K F D K X E W G
A T T K B B K P S R V D Y E T Q G B P L K L N
L R A E R W J H P I A S J Z T S T F G M D V I
T E A M W O R K L N N U E N S H P G M J F M N
U O Q Q E J Y D A G K I Y G B E E U Q E O P E
K V L H K M H U Y J W V B M A P E R O E D B T
R U A I M H E V E N N W L B J R R P U R K V S
F L R C H G L O R Q B N W S S D U Q M F G N I
Q Y P S N M T L W E P F Z Y G I A O V F K M L
B Z J S B Q K F T E P B J X X Z E U C Z D D N
S A E D I F C A R N K O F K L W Y F C N I M M
B R Q Z X R M Y N M Q K J U S U N N C O E A T
I P T C X M E R G E Q D E H X F S U N G E C D
Z O D Q A B D M D J P K W H N A L N Z T X W V
Y P L E V V H R W C C R P S X E G F G H L G P
G R T J J O D N E P B S S Z O T X Y V Z M R W
H G F Q W P V M Y M X S K S P G N O I N I P O
S D H C F I T S A U O A E S I D X W Z N C X H
K A Q X L C I O L F X T J P D R Q O J S Z D P
Z F Q L D H I G E A D F O C F L R Q C J C X J
J Z J H T G E Y Q N Z H D B V W C O W G S K D
```

encourages opinion   teammate
groups   player   teamwork
ideas   sharing   together
job   small
listening   team

CHAPTER 7

How to Succeed in Studying Third Grade History

History might sound like a bunch of stories about the past, but it's so much more! Third grade history is a chance to learn about exciting events, brave people, and even how the world we live in came to be. The good news is that studying history doesn't have to be boring or overwhelming. With the right tips, you can ace your history lessons and even have fun doing it. Here are some ideas and real-life examples to help you succeed in third grade history.

1. Get Curious!

History is all about asking, "What happened?" and "Why did it happen?" When you're curious, you'll want to learn more. For example, if you're learning about Native American tribes, don't just memorize the names of the tribes. Ask questions like:

- "What games did kids play back then?"
- "What kinds of food did they eat?"

By finding answers to these kinds of questions, you'll remember the lesson better and find it more exciting. Imagine your teacher tells you about a famous explorer. Instead of just writing down facts, think, "What would it have been like to sail on that ship?"

2. Make a Timeline

History is all about events happening in order. One excellent way to keep track of what you're learning is to make a timeline. A timeline is like a road map for time.

Let's say your class is studying American history. You can mark events like these on your timeline.

- The signing of the Declaration of Independence.
- The first Thanksgiving.
- When Abraham Lincoln became president.

You can even add little drawings or color-code events to make it fun. For example, draw a turkey for the first Thanksgiving or a tiny hat for Lincoln. This will help you understand what happened first and how everything fits together.

3. Turn History into a Story

Think of history as a big adventure story with heroes, villains, and exciting twists. Instead of just reading about George Washington crossing the Delaware River, imagine what it would have been like to be there. Was it cold? Were the soldiers scared? When you picture history like a story, it's easier to remember.

Here's a real-life example: When learning about the Civil Rights Movement, think of Martin Luther King Jr. as the hero of a big story about fairness and bravery. What was he trying to do? How did people help him? How would you have felt if you were part of that story?

4. Use Visuals to Bring History to Life

Pictures and maps are great tools for studying history. If your teacher talks about a battle, look at a map to see where it happened. If you're learning about ancient Egypt, find pictures of pyramids or hieroglyphs.

Here's a fun idea:
Create a "history gallery" on your bedroom wall. Every time you learn about a new person or event, add a picture, map, or drawing to your gallery. For example, if you're studying Rosa Parks, you could add a picture of a bus and write her name underneath.

5. Play History Games

Studying doesn't always have to mean sitting at a desk. Turn history into a game!

Jeopardy-Style Quiz: Ask a parent or sibling to quiz you on what you've learned. For example, "Who was the first president of the United States?" or "Which country gave the Statue of Liberty to America?"

Act It Out: If you're learning about the Pilgrims, pretend you're on the Mayflower. What would you pack? What would it feel like to sail for weeks?

Games make studying feel more like fun and less like work.

6. Study With Friends

Two (or three) heads are better than one! When you study with friends, you can share ideas and help each other understand tough lessons. For example, if you're learning about the Revolutionary War, one friend could pretend to be a Redcoat while another pretends to be a Patriot. You can take turns quizzing each other or working on projects together.

Pro tip: If you have a big history test coming up, form a study group. You can quiz each other on dates, play history games, or even act out important events. It's a lot more fun than studying alone!

7. Relate History to Your Life

Sometimes history feels far away, but it's actually closer than you think! For example, when learning about pioneers, ask yourself, "What would I pack if I had to travel in a wagon?" Or, when studying the Civil Rights Movement, think about how important it is to treat everyone fairly, even on the playground.

Real-Life Scenario:
Let's say you're learning about the first schools in America. Imagine going to school in a one-room building with kids of all ages. How would it be different from your school today? Thinking about how history connects to your life makes it feel real and important.

8. Don't Be Afraid to Ask Questions

If you don't understand something, it's okay to ask for help. Maybe you're confused about why the American colonies wanted independence or how Harriet Tubman helped so many people. Raise your hand and ask your teacher! Chances are, other kids have the same question.

Pro tip: Write down questions you think of during a lesson. For example, if your teacher mentions the Gold Rush, you might wonder, "How did people know where to find gold?" Asking questions helps you learn and shows your teacher that you're paying attention.

9. Practice Explaining What You Learned

One of the best ways to study history is to teach someone else. After school, tell your family about what you learned that day. For example, if your class studied the Boston Tea Party, explain why it happened and what the colonists did. When you teach others, it helps you remember the information better.

10. Celebrate What You've Learned

When you finish a history unit, take a moment to celebrate! Maybe you can make a craft, like a paper hat from the American Revolution or a diorama of a historic scene. Or, reward yourself with a fun activity, like watching a kid-friendly history video or visiting a local museum.

Conclusion

History is full of amazing stories, and third grade is the perfect time to explore them. By staying curious, using tools like timelines and maps, and making history fun, you can succeed and even enjoy learning about the past. Remember, history isn't just about dates and facts—it's about people, places, and ideas that changed the world. Who knows? Maybe one day someone will be studying your story in history class!

Chapter 7 How to Succeed in Studying Third Grade History

```
Q F H S U W R S E W R I T E G C H E X D J U H
C K Z C O V X U V W C S L S H A S Q P R T V A
W D Q L K N V Z S Q T W D X C U Z R F J X O U
F J P W E K V U T J Z L G X N H K T Z H D N S
Q X M Q X K I K N S T N B Y S V H P O U C U A
M O X M Q O K B M S K Z U Z F U Q X Q N W F N
L K J H I S T O R Y Y H A L T V O Q Y N H M G
I L G Z K E Q Z C S D X Y R Y U V I T W V T G
K E C H F I U W I O U L B O Z I X B R B F E X
P Z M A G V Q R E N T R A P Z Q U R W U B X M
A Q F Y T X J I G M S O T F X A W J F I C X E
K A G I Q U E S T I O N S R T G T E Y Y O P Q
Z T H Y Z A V E M M X I Q V X R W Q G R H X C
X Z P D Y E V N N J R R W X R S V N D S H W L
N D M N Y R O T S I P F V W T S L A U S I V U
C G C L F F Y V O K L Z F U N G S G A X I Z Q
C V M R E A L L I F E E D J K N X R S N X Z R
Z L D X I H U G N B H Y M Q L M S I E G Q F I
V U E U D R D H O W I A R I O J C M M D W A K
H X T M J Y H C V N G M W O T S D F A E A C L
C U Z T K I E T G E U G N N Q B B U G A Y T K
H P V N N C Q P W V W S M W F T I R S V Q S J
I B Q R L Q C H G P L K S Z A M F Z X Z Z N B
```

curious
facts
games
history
partner

questions
reallife (real life)
story
study
studying

timeline
visuals
write

CHAPTER 8

How to Succeed in Studying Third Grade Math

1. Math is Like a Puzzle—Find the Fun

Math might feel like a big challenge, but it's actually like solving puzzles. When you think of it as a game, it becomes way more fun. Imagine you're a detective, and your job is to figure out what 7 + 8 equals. You might even turn math problems into a competition with yourself—how fast can you solve it?

Real-Life Scenario:
You're at lunch and want to split 12 cookies with three friends. Instead of panicking, think of it as a math puzzle: "How many cookies does each person get?" (Hint: It's 4!)

2. Ask Questions Until It Makes Sense

Math is all about understanding, so if something doesn't click, don't be afraid to ask questions. Your teacher is there to help, and chances are, other kids are wondering about the same thing. Asking questions doesn't make you "bad" at math—it makes you smart for wanting to learn more!

Real-Life Scenario:
Your teacher explains fractions, but you're still unsure what "1/4" means. Raise your hand and ask, "Can you show an example with pizza?" Boom! Suddenly, fractions are a lot tastier.

3. Practice Makes Progress

Just like riding a bike or learning to draw, getting good at math takes practice. The more you work on it, the better you'll get. And hey, it's okay to make mistakes, that's how your brain learns!

Pro Tip: Use math apps or games to practice. They make learning feel like playtime instead of homework.

Real-Life Scenario:
You're doing your multiplication homework and keep getting stuck on 6 x 7. Write it down five times, and maybe even create a silly rhyme: "Six times seven, forty-two, math is fun, and so are you!"

4. Make Math Part of Your World

Math is everywhere! When you start looking for it, you'll see math in sports, video games, cooking, and even your favorite shows. Use everyday moments to practice what you've learned in school.

Real-Life Scenario:
You're helping your parents bake cookies, and the recipe calls for 2 cups of flour, but you only have a 1-cup measuring tool. Use addition to figure out how many scoops you need.
(Hint: 1 cup + 1 cup = 2 cups!)

5. Teamwork Makes Math Work

Sometimes, working with a friend or small group can make math easier and more fun. You can share ideas, compare answers, and help each other figure out tricky problems.

Real-Life Scenario:
Your group is solving a word problem: "If there are 24 apples and 6 baskets, how many apples go in each basket?" You suggest dividing the apples, while your friend suggests drawing the baskets. Together, you figure out the answer is 4 apples per basket.

6. Break It Down

Big math problems can feel overwhelming, but breaking them into smaller steps can make them much easier. Think of it like climbing a ladder—one step at a time.

Real-Life Scenario:
The question is, "What is 236 + 157?" First, add the ones place (6 + 7 = 13). Then add the tens place, then the hundreds. Step by step, you'll get the answer: 393.

7. Use Tricks and Shortcuts

Math is full of cool tricks to make problems simpler. Here are a few to try:

The 9 Times Trick:
For 9 times tables, hold up your hands. Fold down the finger for the number you're multiplying (e.g., 9 x 4 = fold down your 4th finger). You'll have 3 fingers on one side and 6 on the other—36!

Doubles Plus One:
If you're solving 7 + 8, think of it as 7 + 7 + 1. Boom, that's 15.

Real-Life Scenario:
You're in a math race, and the question is 9 x 6. Use the finger trick, and you win!

8. Check Your Work

Even math wizards make mistakes, so always double-check your answers. Take a second to go back through your work and make sure everything adds up.

Real-Life Scenario:
You finish a test question: "42 ÷ 6 = ?" At first, you wrote 8. When you check, you realize 8 x 6 = 48, not 42. The real answer is 7. High-five for catching it!

9. Don't Give Up—Be a Math Ninja

Some math problems might feel impossible, but don't let them defeat you. Take a deep breath, try a new strategy, or ask for help. Every problem you solve makes you stronger and smarter.

Real-Life Scenario:

You're learning long division, and it feels like your brain might explode. Instead of giving up, you ask your teacher for another example. Slowly but surely, you'll figure it out—and it's an amazing feeling when you do!

10. Celebrate Your Math Wins

When you get a tough problem right or improve your math grade, take a moment to celebrate! You worked hard, and you deserve to feel proud.

Real-Life Scenario:

You've been practicing subtraction with regrouping and have finally nailed it on your quiz. Treat yourself to a fun activity after school—you earned it!

Final Thought

Math isn't about being perfect; it's about trying, learning, and getting better every day. With practice, teamwork, and a little creativity, you'll be a third-grade math star in no time. So go ahead—grab those numbers and show them who's boss! You are!

Chapter 8 How to Succeed in Studying Third Grade Math

```
H B T A V D Y H J E R D U K H H A D I U F B G
T G K P R A C T I C E M N O F Z G M L E G N B
V L L Z M G F K E R N K S W Z B P Z X O I Z X
O V A I F U M E U E I O W P R M A Q J V D C O
G Z D H P X Y Z F B G S Z D E R M I L I E Z G
Q D O S S X I G O M G H V G W T L O Z M D K D
S Q E U S M L A I E W H C Y X B S J P S W R B
B B P T I L R Z O M K I A L H P R L Q H V V M
I L E J E W P P Q E L U O X T D S G O T E Z E
Q C T F V C N W E R W B I U L E P L D Y Y X W
K I Z N Y S T U N P N M F S Z C B L H Z D F C
M Q R J U X I I X L O L J Z F W S A N X T T X
I S Z N Y S Y R V B A R F X N X W M S S Q Z L
M A T H V R K B R E L L S A I Q V S P K K T P
E C J U X B F N A Y Q U E S T I O N S J H K O
L L I K C D F F M K C C F L Y T P S P V Q L C
O F Z P J T U M G G D A K Y S T T T Z O P X S
I O K Z M L R S K C I R T S D O R Z M G S W D
Y N B O U B X O R T S P T Y S D S K A A E D O
A I K D V P K N H F L P Q M W N O R C P O X E
S S X X U F F T F S P L T S Y H X T I E L C F
C X M M V Q I O E N W I S G L C J F R H H Q N
T O A H Y T G S Z M K W L K L A B Q H G A C Z
```

ask   puzzle   solving
check   questions   steps
detective   remember   tricks
math   shortcuts
practice   small

69

CHAPTER 9

How to Become a Reading Rockstar in Third Grade

Hey there, future reading champ! Third grade is a big year for reading—you'll dive into fun stories, learn cool facts, and discover how reading can take you on amazing adventures. Whether you're reading chapter books, comics, or even recipes, this chapter is here to help you succeed with tons of tips, tricks, and real-life examples. Let's get started!

1. Find Books You Love
Reading is way more enjoyable when you're excited about the book. Look for books about your favorite hobbies, animals, or adventures. It doesn't matter if it's fiction, nonfiction, or even a graphic novel—as long as you love it.

Real-Life Scenario:
You love dinosaurs, so you pick a book about T-Rexes at the library. Suddenly, reading feels like exploring Jurassic Park. Who knew learning about fossils could be so cool?

2. Set Reading Goals
A great way to stay motivated is to set small goals for yourself. Try reading for 15 minutes a day or finishing a certain number of pages each week. Celebrate when you reach your goal!

Real-Life Scenario:
You decide to read three chapters of your favorite book before the weekend. By Friday, you've done it—and you treat yourself to an extra 10 minutes of playtime.

3. Create a Cozy Reading Spot

Having a special spot for reading makes it feel extra fun. Find a comfy chair, add some pillows, and keep your favorite books nearby. You'll be ready to jump into any story.

Real-Life Scenario:
You make a reading fort with blankets in your living room. Inside, you read a mystery book, and it feels like you're solving the case right from your secret hideout.

4. Use Reading Strategies

Don't worry when you're struggling with a word or don't understand something—just use a strategy! Here are some things to try:

Sound it out:
 Break the word into smaller parts.
Look for clues: Check the pictures or read the sentence again to figure out the meaning.
Ask for help: A teacher, parent, or friend can explain words or phrases.

Real-Life Scenario:
You're reading about animals and see the word "nocturnal." You don't know what it means, so you read the next sentence: "Owls and bats are active at night." Ah-ha! Now you know it means being awake at night.

5. Read Aloud and Listen

Reading out loud helps you understand the story better and makes the words stick in your brain. You can also ask someone to read to you, it's fun to hear the story in their voice.

Real-Life Scenario:
You're reading a funny book and sharing it with your little brother. You both laugh when you read the silly voices out loud.

Pro Tip: You're practicing without even realizing it!

6. Join the Conversation

Books are even better when you share them with others. Talk about the characters, plot, or what you think will happen next. It helps you remember the story and understand it better.

Real-Life Scenario:
Your class reads Charlotte's Web. During a group discussion, you say, "I think Charlotte is brave for helping Wilbur." A classmate agrees, and you both talk about your favorite parts.

7. Explore Nonfiction Too

Fictional stories are amazing, but nonfiction can be just as exciting! Nonfiction books teach you about real people, places, and events. You can learn about anything—from sharks to space!

Real-Life Scenario:
Your teacher assigns a book report, and you choose a biography about Harriet Tubman. Learning about her bravery inspires you to share her story with your family.

8. Use the Five-Finger Rule

Not sure if a book is the right level for you? Try this trick: Open to a random page and read it. If there are more than five words you don't know, the book might be too challenging for now. That's okay, save it for later and pick a book that fits just right.

Real-Life Scenario:
You try reading a book about ancient history but don't understand most of the words. Instead, you pick a book about inventors that's easier to read—and way more fun!

9. Practice Every Day

Reading every day helps you get better and faster. Even a few minutes a day can make a big difference. Try reading before bed, during lunch, or whenever you have free time.

Real-Life Scenario:
You keep a book in your backpack and read during car rides. By the end of the week, you've finished a whole chapter book!

10. Learn New Words

Every time you read, you can learn new words. Keep a list of interesting words and their meanings in a notebook. You'll be surprised how quickly your vocabulary grows!

Real-Life Scenario:
While reading a fantasy book, you find the word "enchanted." Just write it down, look it up, and use it in your own stories. "The enchanted forest was filled with glowing trees!"

11. Use Your Imagination

Reading isn't just about words—it's about seeing the story in your mind. Picture the characters, imagine the setting, and think about what's happening.

Real-Life Scenario:
You're reading a book about pirates and imagine yourself sailing the high seas. Suddenly, you feel like you're part of the adventure!

12. Never Give Up

If reading feels difficult sometimes, don't give up! The more you practice, the easier it gets. Everyone improves at their own pace, so keep going and be proud of your progress.

Real-Life Scenario:
You're reading a long chapter book for the first time. At first, it's slow, but by chapter three, you're hooked. By the end, you're so proud you finished a "big kid" book!

Final Thought

Reading isn't just something you do in school, it's a superpower that can take you anywhere. With the right books, some daily practice, and a little imagination, you'll be a third grade reading superstar in no time. So, grab a book and get ready for an amazing adventure—you've got this!

Chapter 9 How to Become a Reading Rockstar in Third Grade

```
K B B U U L L C X B Y Y J U K L T Q F H T M I
N O T Y N Z E D E Y N O B Z H Q E R S W M M A
O I H S Z U J D B B P S B S T R A T E G I E S
J O X O O M F S E R I P Y O X Z X D U O L A Y
P U Q T V O V T A P M Y O Z Z C R D W S N X R
V O C X F V H C E M S J I L O Z U Q K E O J N
Q U X A Q R T S Y I R R R N G C G B T K D G V
O W N U Q I A W R J D A V G S U N S H L B Z J
Q Z O T C U G E S O R E I R L W I E K O F F P
G U N E V N G B R M R K M P A L D I G S D A I
M J F L Q Q N F A S N L U V O O A M U I U N E
P O I Z O G S D A W Y B A E G V E R C V I E H
A B C P K Q G T K G F G B Y A X R I N B Z O T
M C T K K V I P D H J G N O I T A N I G A M I
X Q I W M O E V E R Y D A Y Z F N D Z K T Q A
N L O J N P D M F D Q A U W L H L X O D K E T
G I N P K M X R U Q I H E C A U U H I C M O L
N F T B I U J S B O Z G T Q F K U S F F F F Z
C A W Z D U A B B X H S C O T T K M A W T D T
E X J R L O T U T O J W T B P O H H P V Z Y Q
V V R B R S M G P Z W A J O O S E G H D X C U
J J C C Q D B J G Z T N Z B D S E L N S H X Y
G H O Z G U E A Y Q K L G C E X O R X H R F W
```

aloud
books
conversation
cozy
everyday

goals
imagination
listen
nonfiction
practice

reading
spot
strategies

CHAPTER 10

How to Crush It in Third Grade P.E.

Hey, future athlete! Physical education (P.E.) is more than just running laps or playing dodgeball—it's about having fun, learning new skills, and staying active. Whether you love sports or just enjoy playing games with friends, this chapter will give you tons of ideas and real-life tips to help you succeed in P.E. Let's get moving!

1. Warm Up Like a Champ
Before jumping into any activity, warming up is key. Stretching and doing a few light exercises get your body ready to move and help prevent injuries. Think of it like waking up your muscles for the day.

Real-Life Scenario:
Your teacher says to jog around the gym for two minutes before basketball practice. At first, it feels silly, but by the time you start dribbling the ball, you feel faster and more ready to play.

2. Always Try Your Best

You don't have to be the fastest runner or the best kicker to do well in P.E.. What matters is that you try your hardest. Effort is more important than winning!

Real-Life Scenario:
You're playing kickball, and it's your turn to bat. Even if you don't kick a home run, running as fast as you can to first base shows your team, you're giving it your all.

3. Listen and Learn

P.E. isn't just about playing games, it's also about learning the rules and skills for each sport. Listen carefully when your teacher explains how to play. Knowing the rules makes the game more fun!

Real-Life Scenario:
Your class is learning soccer, and your teacher explains the rule about not touching the ball with your hands. You pay attention and impress everyone by dribbling with your feet like a pro.

4. Be a Team Player
In P.E., you'll often work with teammates. Being a good team player means cheering others on, sharing the ball, and taking turns. Remember, it's not just about you, it's about the whole team.

Real-Life Scenario:
You're playing volleyball, and your teammate misses a serve. Instead of getting upset, you say, "Nice try! You've got this!" Your positive attitude makes everyone feel better and play harder.

5. Practice Makes Perfect
No one is born amazing at sports—it takes practice to get better. If you're not great at something right away, don't worry. Keep trying, and you'll improve over time.

Real-Life Scenario:
You struggle to hit the baseball during practice, but after a few tries and some tips from your coach, you finally make contact. The ball flies, and you feel like a star!

6. Stay Active, Even Off the Field

P.E. is just one part of staying active. Playing outside, riding your bike, or dancing at home all help you stay fit and have fun. The more you move, the better you'll feel in P.E.

Real-Life Scenario:

You start jumping rope at home for fun. The next time your class has a jump rope challenge, you crush it because you've been practicing without even realizing it!

7. Wear the Right Gear

Comfortable clothes and proper shoes make a big difference in P.E. If you're wearing slippery shoes or tight jeans, it'll be harder to move and play your best.

Real-Life Scenario:

It's running day, and you're wearing sneakers instead of sandals. While your friend keeps slipping, you run like the wind because you came prepared.

8. Learn from Mistakes:

Everybody makes mistakes in P.E., whether it's missing a catch or tripping over a hurdle. The important thing is to learn from it and try again. Mistakes are just part of the game.

Real-Life Scenario:

You're playing basketball and miss an easy shot. Instead of getting upset, you focus on your next chance and score a point. Practice makes progress!

9. Respect the Rules

Rules aren't there to ruin the fun, they're there to keep the games fair and safe. Follow them, and you'll have a better time in class.

Real-Life Scenario:

Your class is playing tag, and the rule is "no pushing." You make sure to tag gently and remind others to do the same. Everyone plays safely, and no one gets hurt.

10. Cheer on Your Friends

Encouraging your classmates can make P.E. way more fun. A simple "Good job!" or "You can do it!" goes a long way in making others feel great.

Real-Life Scenario:

Your friend is nervous about climbing the rope. You cheer them on, saying, "You've got this!" They smile, climb higher than they thought they could, and feel proud thanks to your support.

11. Stay Hydrated

P.E. can make you sweat, so don't forget to drink water. Staying hydrated keeps you feeling strong and energized.

Real-Life Scenario:

After a tough game of soccer, you grab your water bottle and take a big gulp. You feel refreshed and ready for the next activity.

12. Cool Down Afterward

Just like warming up, cooling down is important. Stretching after P.E. helps your body recover and keeps your muscles from feeling sore.

Real-Life Scenario:

After running sprints, your teacher leads the class in stretching. You touch your toes and feel your legs relaxed and ready for the rest of your day.

13. Keep a Positive Attitude

Not every day in P.E. will be perfect. You might lose a game or feel tired, but staying positive will help you enjoy the class more.

Real-Life Scenario:

Your team doesn't win during relay races, but you high-five your teammates and say, "We'll get them next time!" Suddenly, it feels like a win anyway.

14. Try New Things

P.E. is a great chance to try sports and activities you've never done before. Even if it feels weird at first, give it a shot—you might discover something you love.

Real-Life Scenario:

Your class is learning how to play badminton, and you've never used a racket before. At first, you miss the birdie, but by the end of class, you're hitting it like a champ.

Final Thought

P.E. is about having fun, staying active, and learning new skills. By trying your best, being a good teammate, and staying positive, you'll become a third-grade P.E. superstar. So, lace up your sneakers, grab some water, and get ready to move—you've got this!

Chapter 10 How to Crush It in Third Grade P.E.

```
X S C I V G H I X O M B A C D T G I K K Y C O
X U F F H P D W R N G L M Q V V Z E M P E E Y
F D H N W W F N P Q P I Y D Y X M H H F E Z Z
B W N Z Q Z M A V V B Y R M D W C Y D B K A Q
Y B T C A X S M O R Z U S V V M S A O G F C M
C R I I Z B K F D K A E Y G Y I T T G S C E W
Q O A M W G W N J K E Z T S C F Z Q B B U D S
X H X I W C O C O M Y E M A P R N G U V F M O
Q W V U O R E L P I S D L Z L M S O H W N F U
L K W V J R O Z G F T D U A R R O G M A A R F
B Q B E H U Q F O V F A U W R T E L A T A S M
T I E L F X S K I N C M C R R M L I S E G K N
R W O Z V P F W D Y F B U U Q D N E G M B F E
I E K Y P R R K J G M L H V D V I L A L B L C
R A Y X I U Z P V K E K J M A E T S V R V A I
J K E A S U V H A S R T S T I A F D D S N V T
P Q H B L B R L T T P W G E L T W E R S T N C
C J Q I Y P I V Q B W W C Z I A T L R W R S A
E C A V E S M Y B T N H H I R A A Y S R O R R
I N I L T G H Q M O Y K H M R K H T X F F R P
E U O E Z W A H T F F Y U D X I I Y R W F O W
O G N R U R S J D U S P Y S K A S S J B E L S
P J G T U W J T B N B H R N D N N H U C P Z B
```

education   learn   rules
effort   listen   team
fun   physical   warmup
gear   player
hydrated   practice

CHAPTER 11

How to Be a Science Superstar in Third Grade

Hey, future scientist! Third grade science is all about exploring the world around you, asking big questions, and finding out cool answers. Whether you're studying plants, animals, weather, or even outer space, this chapter will help you succeed with fun tips, real-life examples, and ideas you can use every day. Let's dive in—science style!

1. Start with Curiosity

Science is all about being curious. If you've ever wondered, "Why is the sky blue?" or "How do birds fly?" you're already thinking like a scientist. In third grade, use that curiosity to explore new topics and stay excited about learning.

Real-Life Scenario:
You're studying plants in class, and you notice that some flowers on the playground grow in the sun while others grow in the shade. Ask yourself, "Why is that?" and bring your observation to class—it might just spark a great discussion.

2. Pay Attention During Experiments

Experiments are one of the most exciting parts of science! When your teacher sets up an activity, like testing which objects sink or float, pay close attention to the steps. Following directions carefully will help you get the best results.

Real-Life Scenario:
Your teacher gives your group a cup of water, a paperclip, a rock, and a cork. Before tossing everything in, you predict which will float. When the cork floats, you learn about buoyancy—and you can tell your classmates why their guesses might have been different.

3. Keep a Science Journal

Scientists write everything down, and you can too! Use a science journal to track what you learn, draw diagrams, or write down questions. It's like your own personal book of discoveries.

Pro Tip: Use colored pencils to draw pictures of experiments like a growing plant or a volcano erupting. Adding color makes it more fun and easier to understand later.

Real-Life Scenario:
You're learning about the water cycle and drawing a diagram of evaporation, condensation, and precipitation in your journal. Later, when it rains, you look back at your notes and feel like a weather expert.

4. Ask Questions—Lots of Them

The best scientists always ask questions. If you don't understand something or want to know more, speak up! There's no such thing as a silly question in science.

Real-Life Scenario:
Your teacher shows a video about animals that hibernate, and you wonder, "Do fish hibernate too?" You ask the question in class, and your teacher explains that some fish slow down in cold water. Now you know something extra cool!

5. Learn Through Hands-On Activities

Science isn't just reading from a textbook, it's about doing! Whether it's building a model of the solar system or growing beans in a cup, these activities help you understand science better by seeing it in action.

Real-Life Scenario:
Your class is studying gravity, and your teacher asks you to drop different objects—a ball, a feather, and a pencil. You notice the feather falls more slowly, and you learn about air resistance. Doing it yourself makes the lesson unforgettable.

6. Work Well with Your Group

Science projects often involve teamwork. When you're in a group, listen to everyone's ideas, share your own, and divide tasks so everyone gets to participate.

Real-Life Scenario:
Your group is building a model of a habitat for a desert animal. One person gathers pictures of cacti, another adds sand to the shoebox, and you draw a lizard. When the project is done, it's amazing because everyone worked together.

7. Use Your Senses

Science is all about observing the world around you. Use your eyes, ears, nose, and even touch (safely!) to gather information.

Real-Life Scenario:
Your class goes outside to study leaves. You notice some are smooth, some are rough, and some have funny smells. Using your senses helps you figure out how different trees survive in different places.

8. Stay Organized

Science involves a lot of materials, papers, notebooks, and experiment supplies. Keep your science stuff organized so you can easily find what you need.

Pro Tip: Use folders or a special section in your binder for science handouts and notes.

Real-Life Scenario:
Your teacher asks you to review your notes on the states of matter. You open your science folder, and there's your chart showing solids, liquids, and gases. Easy!

9. Watch the World Around You

The best part about science is that it's everywhere! Pay attention to things like the weather, animals, and how things work in your daily life. The more you observe, the better you'll understand science.

Real-Life Scenario:
You're eating breakfast and notice steam rising from your hot cocoa. You realize it's an example of evaporation. Who knew science could happen at the breakfast table?

10. Use Technology for Extra Learning

There are so many cool apps, videos, and websites about science. If you're curious about volcanoes or stars, find a video or game that teaches you more.

Real-Life Scenario:
Your class learns about the solar system, and you want to know more about black holes. At home, you watch a fun video explaining how they form. The next day, you share what you learned with your classmates.

11. Practice for Tests the Fun Way
Studying for science tests doesn't have to be boring. Make flashcards, quiz yourself, or ask a parent or friend to help. Try acting out what you've learned; pretend you're a raindrop traveling through the water cycle or a butterfly going through metamorphosis.

Real-Life Scenario:
You and a friend are studying for a test on ecosystems. You quiz each other about the difference between producers, consumers, and decomposers. When you ace the test, you know teamwork paid off.

12. Never Give Up
Science can get tricky sometimes, but don't let that stop you. If you don't understand something, ask for help, watch a video, or try looking at it a different way. Every great scientist had to work through tough problems, just like you.

Real-Life Scenario:
You're trying to memorize the parts of a plant but keep mixing up "stamen" and "stem." Your teacher suggests drawing a labeled diagram. Suddenly, it all makes sense!

Final Thought
Science is an adventure waiting to happen. By staying curious, working hard, and having fun with experiments, you'll become a third-grade science superstar. So, grab your goggles and get ready to explore—you've got this!

Chapter 11 How to Be a Science Superstar in Third Grade

```
F M K D Y T D W W D T K X J T Y W C B P I W T
V H Y Q O V O R F W F T S F V N R S R P P J S
M W A H H Z E T S E Y S K B T C Y C L I B E R
Y P M V A K J G U O A N D F Z X N I I O L O O
R I V F W U J A U W U O M I N C U R Y G P L A
V N Y C U D Z Q A Z R I K S D J O G G Y H T L
G U Q F T J P J V A C T C P Z G O O Q P V N S
N H W U W X X D Q F E S W W B L G X S R E P I
R A T S R E P U S T D E E D O X W F Q R Q U K
V E Q V E I Z V J E M U J N H M D R N S Y C A
Z C U R I O S I T Y N Q H P L J R F F Q R W R
E X P E R I M E N T S C N U P F G C L K K P M
A W B C I Z S R S A E F G C B W H A N D S O N
F C C B I M P T O T G A E K Z G Q V U D F B M
S M H O H L O X O Q O R I S K R T X O R F W S
U P J U Q L V W B N P J O T L K Z J D T A W E
S M W P A M V W L H W H U W X V C E Y T P W P
E L V A J D H A Y T N G Z S T V X R C D M P A
N N I S W G N L F P R C R J A F R H W W S R S
S X C V B R K R D O Q J R B W S W D P X X X T
E T G V U I Z B U C G I D Y C Y R S B L C Z N
S N Q O Z Y Q P L V H F C G F P E C N E I C S
L I J M V I T D X B N S V T B Q C C D P A Q T
```

curiosity
experiments
goggles
group
handson (hands on)

journal
organize
questions
science
senses

superstar
technology
watch

CHAPTER 12

How to Rock Third Grade Writing

Hey there, future author! Writing in third grade can be a lot of fun. Whether you're creating stories, writing about real-life stuff, or even just answering questions in class, this chapter is packed with ideas to help you succeed. Writing doesn't have to be hard; it's like telling your thoughts on paper. Let's get started and make writing your superpower!

1. Start with an Idea

Every great piece of writing starts with an idea. Don't worry if you can't think of something right away—ideas are everywhere! Look around, think about your favorite things, or imagine something wild and fun.

Real-Life Scenario:
Your teacher asks you to write about your favorite day. At first, you're stuck. Then you remember your trip to the zoo where a monkey threw a banana, and suddenly you can't stop writing.

2. Use a Plan

Before you start writing, make a plan. You can use a graphic organizer, jot down notes, or make a quick list. A plan helps your ideas stay organized, so your writing is clear.

Real-Life Scenario:
Your teacher asks you to write a story about an adventure. You make a quick plan:

- **Beginning:** A kid finds a treasure map.
- **Middle:** They face a scary snake in the jungle.
- **End:** They find the treasure and share it with their friends.

With your plan ready, the story practically writes itself!

3. Write in Complete Sentences

A sentence has to have a subject (who or what) and a verb (action). Make sure your sentences are clear and make sense. If you're not sure, read them out loud to check.

Real-Life Scenario:
You're writing about your weekend. Instead of writing "Park fun," you write, "I went to the park, and we had so much fun playing on the swings." See the difference? Complete sentences make your writing shine.

4. Add Details to Bring It to Life

Great writing makes readers feel like they're right there with you. Use details to describe what you see, hear, feel, taste, or smell.

Real-Life Scenario:
You're writing about eating ice cream. Instead of saying, "It was good," you write, "The chocolate ice cream was cold, creamy, and so sweet it made my tongue tingle." Now your readers are drooling!

5. Use Transition Words
Transition words like first, next, then, and finally help your writing flow smoothly. They guide the reader from one idea to the next.

Real-Life Scenario:
Your teacher asks you to write about your morning routine. You write:

- **First,** I brush my teeth.
- **Next,** I eat breakfast.
- **Then,** I pack my backpack.
- **Finally,** I headed to school.

Easy to follow, right?

6. Practice Spelling and Punctuation

Good spelling and punctuation make your writing easy to read. If you're not sure how to spell a word, check a dictionary or ask for help. Don't forget periods, question marks, and capital letters where they belong.

Real-Life Scenario:
You write, "Did you see the rainbow? It was so pretty." Your teacher reminds you to add punctuation, so it becomes, "Did you see the rainbow? It was so pretty!" Perfect!

7. Edit Like a Pro

After you finish writing, don't stop! Read it again to see if anything needs fixing. Look for spelling mistakes, missing words, or places where you could add more details.

Real-Life Scenario:
You write a story about a dog who saves the day, but when you read it over, you notice you forgot to say how the dog saved the day. You add, "The dog barked loudly to warn the family about the fire." Now it's even better!

8. Try Different Types of Writing

Third grade writing isn't just about stories. You might write poems, book reports, persuasive essays, or even instructions. Each type is unique and trying them all helps you grow as a writer.

Real-Life Scenario:
Your teacher asks you to write instructions for making a sandwich. You write:

Get two slices of bread.
Spread peanut butter on one slice.
Spread jelly on the other.
Put the slices together.

Your classmates try it, and it works perfectly. Success!

9. Read to Write Better

The more you read, the better your writing will get. Books, magazines, or even comics can teach you new words, ideas, and styles.

Real-Life Scenario:
You're reading a mystery book and notice how the author uses clues to build suspense. The next time you write a story, you add a secret map and a locked treasure chest. Your story gets rave reviews from your teacher!

10. Share Your Writing

Sharing your writing with others helps you feel proud of your work. Read it to a friend, show it to your teacher, or even present it to the class.

Real-Life Scenario:
You write a poem about a thunderstorm and read it to your family. They clap and say, "Wow, you're a great poet!" Suddenly, writing feels even more awesome.

11. Learn from Feedback

When your teacher or friends give you tips to improve your writing, listen carefully. It's not about being perfect, it's about getting better.

Real-Life Scenario:
Your teacher says, "Great story, but you could add more dialogue to make it exciting." You rewrite it with a conversation between the characters, and it really brings the story to life.

12. Keep Practicing

The more you write, the easier it gets. Keep a journal, write letters to your family, or create silly stories just for fun. Every bit of practice helps.

Real-Life Scenario:
You start a journal about your day-to-day adventures. After a few weeks, you notice your sentences are longer, your ideas are clearer, and your stories are more fun to read.

Final Thought
Writing is like magic, it lets you share your ideas, dreams, and stories with the world. By practicing, adding details, and learning new skills, you'll become a third-grade writing superstar in no time. So, grab your pencil and notebook and let your imagination fly! You've got this!

Chapter 12 How to Rock Third Grade Writing

```
R D R T G P X A W W S D G V O R T R C J O T I
I O I M A G I N A T I O N G S L G T O P Z B L
S K A P A S C D C Z R R F U S V O N E T S S W
G A F N P D K K N U U A X M P Q B Z I K C C L
Z C K D Z R W X G E A V N M X W T Q Q V S X I
C U V G R O C X P N L Z Y S R N Q Y C A O V A
I G G I U W N P C I L I I S I N M M L J E K Q
A X U F S E N T E N C E S C F T B G M C F D S
C P K P K U K Z U P P Q N K W Y I I G I M P I
J Q B N I T Y P V K Z C G Z T B F O W X O Q D
W N G D R R A L Y N X S S N Z I I B N P D V J
U N Y S B Q P Z E R A H S U I H W D U O M Y F
F I H D I Z I Q T R C L O H H T D G T I D E R
K C A B D E E F Q B Q A P J L R I X Y B V O G
P H M A E I W H A S X C O S X A I R E I I V K
I L X V T P E R S U A S I V E J F P W L Z W M
N Q C V A U K Z P Q V R Q U H E L E A M J M
U Q S E I E O H X E V O M U H Q P O G R V P S
M C P L L R I D A F E J M Q Q E D J T G T R Q
F Y W R S G N W W X I F N L P R A C T I C E P
Y N K S A T W A Z L A I Q F Z O X Q L T A C T
A S G B H W C D J Z W B K P V A E B C H F J B
K X J N Z X N X D T E S J G A B T U J N J T Q
```

details	persuasive	transition
edit	plan	words
feedback	practice	writing
idea	sentences	
imagination	share	

105

CHAPTER 13

How to Conquer Third Grade Homework

Hey there, homework hero! Third grade is an exciting year, but let's be real—homework isn't always the most enjoyable part. Fortunately, there's good news! With the right tips and tricks, homework can be way easier and even kind of fun! This chapter is full of ideas and real-life examples to help you crush your assignments like a pro. Let's dive in and get to work!

1. Set Up a Homework Spot

Having a special place for homework makes a big difference. Find a quiet, comfy spot where you can focus. Keep your pencils, erasers, and other supplies nearby so you don't have to hunt for them.

Real-Life Scenario:
You usually do homework at the kitchen table, but today your little brother is singing loudly. You decide to move to your bedroom desk, and suddenly, you can focus much better. Problem solved!

2. Make a Homework Schedule

Homework feels less stressful when you plan time for it. Decide if you want to do it right after school, before dinner, or even after a quick play break. Sticking to a schedule helps you stay on track.

Real-Life Scenario:
You get home from school and feel tired, so you take a 15-minute snack break. Then, you start your homework at 4:00 PM every day. By dinnertime, you're done and ready to relax.

3. Start with the Hard Stuff

Do the trickiest assignment first while your brain is fresh. Once the hard part is out of the way, the rest will feel easier.

Real-Life Scenario:
You have a math worksheet, a spelling list, and a reading log. Math feels the hardest, so you tackle it first. After you finish, the spelling and reading seem like a breeze.

4. Break It into Smaller Steps

Big homework assignments can feel overwhelming but breaking them into smaller chunks makes them easier to handle. Take one step at a time!

Real-Life Scenario:
Your teacher asks you to write a paragraph about your favorite animal.
- First, you brainstorm ideas.
- Next, you write three sentences about what it eats.
- Then, you add two more sentences about where it lives.

Before you know it, your paragraph is done!

5. Eliminate Distractions

Homework time should be focused time. Turn off the TV, put away your tablet, and let your family know you need some quiet. Fewer distractions mean you'll finish faster.

Real-Life Scenario:
You start your homework while your sister watches a loud cartoon. You grab headphones to block out the noise and finish your work twice as fast. Nice move!

6. Ask for Help When You Need It

If you're stuck, don't be afraid to ask for help. Your parents, siblings, or even a friend might be able to explain something in a way that makes sense.

Real-Life Scenario:
You don't understand a question on your science worksheet. Instead of guessing, you ask your dad to explain. He shows you an example, and suddenly it clicks. Teamwork for the win!

7. Take Short Breaks

It's hard to stay focused for a long time. If you have a lot of homework, take a 5-minute break after every 20 minutes of work. Stretch, grab a snack, or do a quick dance before getting back to it.

Real-Life Scenario:
You've been working on your math homework for 20 minutes and feel tired. You take a break to do jumping jacks and then come back feeling energized to finish the rest.

8. Double-Check Your Work

Before you pack up your homework, take a few minutes to review it. Check for spelling, neatness, and any mistakes. It's a great habit that helps you do your best.

Real-Life Scenario:
You finish your spelling words but notice you accidentally wrote "beet" instead of "beat." You fix it before handing in your work and feel proud of your attention to detail.

9. Make It Fun

Homework doesn't have to be boring. Use colorful pens, create silly rhymes to remember facts, or turn your assignments into games.

Real-Life Scenario:
You're studying for a spelling quiz and make up a song using your words. Singing "C-H-O-C-O-L-A-T-E, I love chocolate!" makes studying way more fun—and helps you remember.

10. Stay Organized

Keeping your homework organized makes life easier. Use a folder to keep assignments together and write down due dates in a planner or notebook.

Real-Life Scenario:
You forget your reading log one day because it got lost in your backpack. After that, you use a special folder for homework, and you never lose an assignment again. Genius!

11. Reward Yourself

Give yourself a little reward after finishing homework. Maybe it's extra playtime, a favorite snack, or a fun activity. Rewards make homework feel worth it.

Real-Life Scenario:
You promise yourself 15 minutes of your favorite video game after finishing your reading and math. The reward motivates you to focus and finish quickly.

12. Turn It in On Time

Doing your homework is awesome, but turning it in is just as important. Make sure it's packed in your folder or backpack the night before, so you don't forget.

Real-Life Scenario:
You finish your science project, but you forget it on the kitchen counter. After that, you make a habit of putting completed homework straight into your backpack before bed.

13. Learn From Mistakes

If you get something wrong, don't worry! Mistakes are part of learning. When your teacher gives feedback, use it to get better next time.

Real-Life Scenario:
Your teacher marks a math problem wrong and shows you the correct way to solve it. Instead of feeling upset, you practice the steps and get it right on your next homework.

14. Keep a Positive Attitude

Homework might not be your favorite thing, but it helps you practice what you learn in school. Try to think of it as a challenge instead of a chore.

Real-Life Scenario:
You have a lot of homework one night and feel frustrated. Then you remember, "Practice makes me better." You finish your work feeling proud of your offort.

Final Thought

Homework is your chance to show what you know and practice new skills. With a good plan, some focus, and a little fun, you'll be a third-grade homework superstar. So, grab your pencil, set up your spot, and get ready to crush it—you've got this!

Chapter 13 How to Conquer Third Grade Homework

```
U F R E O F C Q W W W E U B B B D P W W B D I
C K R O O B C A Z R T U P R E W A R D X U M O
P Q A T C H Y Z N A E Y D A E F A O E G Q E Z
E U N T V A C I N D Z E Y I L K W D E R F I N
D T A S S O Y I B D F N K I B N A K D C Z S W
Y A E M Q J M T R H I N R G A I L M Q W X V U
L T U U F I U P V M F Z Z N Y A Z G H P J U M
C S L X L R H A S W J A Q C O V Q A O H H S C
O U W E N O Z X S Y W Y G W J N J N R A V X O
P D S I S K K S B T F J R S N D J S F C W O H
Q U N V P P Y W O I N Z F K E X E U R N L J L
G Y X I U Y X I R W M U A S A D J Q C J Z R K
Y V R C B N D S B Q P W K B I Y Q S B E G W F
T W H V R C O V B Q X Y K S B T D Q I C V M D
H G O X E L O X D F L E T C S F L O Z A Y H Y
Z K Q I A Z I K X F D R Y G U A C S U L N H M
E Y D X K B P L K J A A J F Y H H N B P C E R
E S K U S F T C Y C P L E H O F O B C O Q A O
K S G C Z A B V T L Q Z H O L S L M D S D M A
C L G W E F G I H O M E W O R K Z P U O I G Q
A Q Y V Z H O W H W M Y S E L U D E H C S C J
H S C Q I N C F I X V H N O R G A N I Z E J F
K O K Y S F C O U W K Z G R O E R U Z L E W I
```

ask	enjoyable	reward
breaks	help	schedule
check	homework	turnin (turn in)
distractions	organize	
eliminate	place	

CHAPTER 14

How to Be an Exam-Ready Rockstar in Third Grade

Hey, superstar! Exams might sound a little scary, but don't worry—you've got this! Studying for exams is just like getting ready for a big game or performance. The more you practice and prepare, the greater your confidence will become. This chapter is packed with tips, tricks, and real-life examples to help you crush those third-grade exams. Let's get started!

1. Know What's on the Test
Before you start studying, find out what will be on the test. Ask your teacher if you're unsure. Knowing what to focus on will make studying much easier.

Real-Life Scenario:
Your teacher tells you the math test will cover addition, subtraction, and multiplication. Instead of practicing everything, you focus on those topics. Now you're ready for the exact questions you'll see!

2. Make a Study Plan

Break your studying into smaller parts so you don't feel overwhelmed. Study a little each day instead of cramming everything the night before.

Real-Life Scenario:
Your science test is in five days.
- On Monday, you review your notes about plants.
- On Tuesday, you practice the parts of a flower.
- By Friday, you're ready for the whole test because you studied bit by bit.

3. Create a Cozy Study Spot
Find a quiet, comfy place where you can focus. Keep your pencils, erasers, and any study tools you need nearby so you're not running around looking for them.

Real-Life Scenario:
You set up a study spot at the dining table with your books, a notebook, and a cup of water. It feels like your special zone to conquer exams!

4. Use Flashcards for Quick Practice
- Flashcards are a fun and easy way to practice facts and vocabulary. Supplies Needed: Index cards (any size of your choice)
- Write a question or term on one side of an index card and the answer on the flip side.
- After creating the flashcard, read the question and then the answer.
- Read both sides of the card without trying to memorize the answer.
- Repeat the above step over and over
- Do this repeatedly each day. Soon you'll realize that you know the information without really trying to memorize it.
- Test yourself or ask a friend or family member to quiz you.
- **THIS WORKS!**

Real-Life Scenario:
You make flashcards for your spelling test. One card says "enough," and when you flip it over, you've written the definition and how to spell it. You repeat this process repeatedly. By the end of the day, you're a spelling champ!

5. Turn Studying into a Game

Who says studying can't be fun? Turn it into a game by timing yourself, making challenges, or earning points for correct answers.

Real-Life Scenario:
You and your friend play multiplication games. Every time you get a question right, you move your game piece forward on a board. By the end, you're winning—and ready for your math test!

6. Review Your Class Notes

Your teacher gives you clues about the test during lessons. Review your notes to remember important points and key details.

Real-Life Scenario:
You're studying for a history test and go back to your notebook. You see a star next to the sentence: "George Washington was the first president." You realize it's probably important—and you're right!

7. Use Practice Questions

Ask your teacher or parent for practice questions to test yourself. Practicing how to answer questions will make the real test feel easier.

Real-Life Scenario:
Your teacher gives a practice sheet for your fractions test. You work on it at home, and when the test comes, you recognize some of the same types of questions. Score!

8. Take Breaks to Recharge

Studying for hours straight can make your brain feel tired. Take short breaks to rest, stretch, or grab a snack.

Real-Life Scenario:
You study for 20 minutes, then take a 5-minute break to play with your dog. When you come back, you feel refreshed and ready to tackle the next subject.

9. Use Fun Memory Tricks

Tricks like rhymes, songs, or acronyms can help you remember tricky facts. The sillier, the better; it helps the information stick!

Real-Life Scenario:
You're trying to remember the planets in order. Try using this sentence: "My Very Excited Mom Just Slipped Us Nachos" (Mercury, Venus, Earth, Mars, Jupiter, Saturn, Uranus, Neptune). Now you'll never forget!

10. Study With a Buddy

Sometimes, studying with a friend makes it more fun and helps you learn better. You can quiz each other, share tips, or explain things to each other.

Real-Life Scenario:
You and your classmate study spelling together. You quiz each other by saying the word, and whoever spells it right first gets a point. By the end, you've both learned all the words—and had fun, too!

11. Get a Good Night's Sleep

Staying up late to study might sound like a good idea, but your brain needs rest to do its best. So, get a good night's sleep before the exam.

Real-Life Scenario:
You go to bed early before your math test. The next morning, you feel rested and ready to tackle those multiplication problems.

12. Eat a Brain-Boosting Snack

Snacks like fruits, nuts, or yogurt can give your brain energy. Avoid sugary snacks that might make you feel tired later.

Real-Life Scenario:
Before your test, you eat a banana and drink some water. You feel alert and focused during the exam—and you ace it!

13. Stay Calm and Confident

Feeling nervous before a test is normal, but don't let it stop you. Take deep breaths and remind yourself of all the hard work you've done.

Real-Life Scenario:
You start to feel jittery before your reading test. You take three deep breaths and think, "I've got this—I've studied hard!" Suddenly, you feel calm and ready to focus.

12. Eat a Brain-Boosting Snack

Snacks like fruits, nuts, or yogurt can give your brain energy. Avoid sugary snacks that might make you feel tired later.

Real-Life Scenario:
Before your test, you eat a banana and drink some water. You feel alert and focused during the exam—and you ace it!

13. Stay Calm and Confident

Feeling nervous before a test is normal, but don't let it stop you. Take deep breaths and remind yourself of all the hard work you've done.

Real-Life Scenario:
You start to feel jittery before your reading test. You take three deep breaths and think, "I've got this—I've studied hard!" Suddenly, you feel calm and ready to focus.

14. Check Your Work

When you finish your test, use any extra time to check your answers. Look for small mistakes or questions you might have skipped.

Real-Life Scenario:
You finish your science test early and go back to review. You realize you forgot to label one part of the plant diagram and fix it just in time.

Final Thought

Studying for exams doesn't have to be stressful. With the right plan, fun strategies, and a positive attitude, you'll feel confident and ready to shine. So, grab your notebook, practice those questions, and show your tests who's boss. You've got this!

Chapter 14 How to Be an Exam-Ready Rockstar in Third Grade

```
P R S X D S W O S J K T M X B K G I C B N S R
K I X Y J Y C C P A X O U E A U A B F J N R M
A Z V Y B E Y Y Z Z H P C Y M Q K S J O L C A
E A C I E Q O P O R C S X N R O Q W I W N F S
K G Z A J T P S E F W T K E S W R T J K L C D
L E O E G D B N L P Q B Z Z P C S Y O A B X B
V H N J K B T G R F S Z B P V E V L S A U X K
X W P F A R X A Z M U K X C U S B H C R R J P
Q J W E A Q C P Q Z B K A Q T N C D Y G P G A
E Q E P O T U H A Z L D S E R A K W F G G C N
C G L N I H F Z G R Q L H Z R L Q V S Q P S L
J V D C C G E P E N B U K D N B Y L H Y R F X
R S E L K O R L H H A G S Z P Y E G V M Y B R
M A X E J R Z A G W D H F T D E Z M S O V J E
X P H V Y V S N G T D H P H P Q K F Q E N E A
U W A I G P K J W V G V R W S G C W N H T J I
E W E T B V E M E M J S U E S T N A W V U O S
Z J Z O R B F K W Q Z E G K G W U H E X K G N
M Z E T N W Z P G P F A Q N H Q T D E T Q X B
P U Q F B Y K N Q S S U A E C B U H Y K X N T
L X C S M L X G R W Z P L E A T Y X W F R M Z
K G F R G J V A M P G V O U I M Q K O S Z V Z
Y K T B K J I Y L P T T O Y K N Q I Z I N V
```

breaks	notes	sleep
eat	partner	spot
exam	plan	study
flashcards	practice	
memory	questions	

Word Search Solutions

Chapter 1 The Big Day: Conquering the First Day of Third Grades

```
V F R S O R M F S E I L P P U S W H X H J V J
L J T X E J N A P X W I Q Z M I P Y V K Q R W
I L Y C S B V Y C U R I O U S M M I B L F H B
M Z E P U B Q O L F U D E R Y A C B U L K V G
G S G U B T T N L D I E K J S F M P R A C F A
S Q V M M Z U C R P N K H O O Y X M E U D A C
J S V U Y Z Y X W B H E U L W Z R A C G R D Y
A B S A F N S C W R V P I K I E C P Z H U P O
W L M Z D N F Q O P F X A R K R L F J S O E
K T S I Q U Y N W J G K M A F Q Y P K U N K C
P G F R S D H A D O W L E A U T Z T U Q N S Q
T H Y E I D R L C T I R Z C K P L R L P A M L
H P L I K U O F G L B T E V U E H R C H R I R
I U I T H G V I B E I F G E N I T U O R P L H
R K Q F N B K G C O I N D S Z M G T J Y X E B
D P L A D J L I W R G E N L U N C H T I M E V
G G G T W Y Z B S Q C N Q K O A A Q I P C G R
R S Z T R G I T P X R W E U V F K Y L D L T V
A U U B E C D N I R H Q G H C Q F X G M A V T
D A A Q B A M W O H N F B R W A F B O W K U J
E G J U Y L O M F W P W H Q X L F O N U V O S
G T E I Z U F Y P I E O X U T X U T Z U O M R
D D P V I A C O N Q U E R D E N V P T D X Q F
```

Chapter 2 How to Pick the Right Friends in Third Grade

```
G R D I G B A C Q L P S Y X D Y F H A E S V L
G Z Y T I L A U Q Y R D L D T F I N Z B J J Z
Z A O U P X T L G N G R M T W D F U U B I M G
Z Y K M E T S L U D R B V W U Z W F V C T Y E
R X R O P C E T I F D R B B R N O M L L H F M
R N L V W U N Q E B T Y M H D Q T M Y R X E C
H D N E I F O Y X F H E B L L G Q X P Z H O
S F J O P T H Y B W A P G O Z K G Q Y R P Y N
T D X N P K I N D N E S S U L E U O H N I A A
R I N E U C V A H A X X L Q O H V M J Q H B H
D X S E T D Y S A J V N L R A H O X E L S D A
N W H E I N N X X K E T O Z T H T E U C D B M
V P U C G R L B O B N Y Z I P Z Q W V M N N C
F T H K R B F C J P X J G Y P M B L A H E X V
M Y N M D G T W F I Q I U W Q N T Y H V I O J
X R F L D B V B E L E P P D D W C Y K U R X V
C I G F U G X U S X B B M W P D O Q M G E C J
F G Z L H I R A O M E F U N H N L H X X O L C
F H L U W H M Z G O C V D B D H P F W M J R J
J T R B O P Y F T E E L B A T R O E M O C M Z
W C C Z S Q C M F N E T S I L O V P A U C
I Y C O K E S Q K K Y U C C I R N B H Q O C Y
V Y F F H H C K I V V T F L Y B F P U O M R R
```

Chapter 3 How to Handle Disagreements in the Third Grade Classroom

```
I D J N R V V R Y O H I D B C F B T G K S I Z
T N H E E J I U U C S D I N Q W N H Q P X N G
J K L N W Y N E O T C W F B E J C R R U B X F
Z A L F E B S M A W A D S O E V A W F D Q O M
X Z U L N O P T D I S A G R E E M E N T G R Z
V O E E V R E E P G J U J U W G G L S H W F G
M P P P O M D D S B J T N R J Q C H V P H H W
M U W M E Z I P B L X E G R F L L D Y D J Z T
S E I N F I F H N E Y Y V M R A Q F U R H M Z
D S T F O R G I V E N E S S H E N T Z O U I C
E S P U T D R U H X W K E Z Q T S N L L Q C L
Z E M O T I O N M T W X H M Y K Q P L G R Y U
U V K Y A H W G V W P C Y M L U Q W E N Q L F
B R Q R O O C I N R G X B E W A J Z Y C L H M
D O T P W B O G E H I L G L M G C R P A T E M
J M G Q B M P S H M U L S B I O N Y C W K L C
F Q G T J Y S O H U P Q J O C O O H A P V P P
D M B Z A S C Z V Q I C Q R X C I E D T Y C J
E Y U H J O D Z I A C F E P Z T N W Y M S G N
Q S X B X T I F F D P T C F J E I O I Y S R P
Q O M U V V F I U R P A C E E W P O P J A R T
M H L W Q L B V P L S N H B O C O X Q E D E J
T W W I O Y Z W S Y Y E M U J T L M L J K A J
```

Chapter 4 How to Handle Disagreements on the Playground

```
W N D U K P G D M A E W Z H M Z P R O U M P R
K N W N H A H Q M U D T U L M M P Y G Y K K K
K B F D R P H P Y A W A K L A W N W L U Q R G
J D D E O E O G Q V N N I N A Y G Z G V N Y B
U C B R S R W I C H R V B V D V H O L J N J Y
D M S S I V U C L A O D L O M G H L L Q J A K
U C F T V Z B P W M Z K U L H H Z R T M T I C
S B X A R Y E T F R B I F K Q C I E Q M L K O
V R Y N E C L G Z Y S I E V I T C E P S R E P
A A E D P H M W U N I S M L V H J L O O C Q B
Y J Y C U X A O R G Q R P H B W A Y G H P V X
S B P X S A K U T L K I F Q L Y U Y I P W P Z
G B K K J V T H Q M F D V Y G X I L V Q A P
Q Z Q E E G T X H W Q W D R S L M P R L S Y F
B V I O N A Y G S T O G O A O A X B O G C J T
U B P I L E S P E D H U B Q P N J I C Q I B N
T X K O T H I Q U V N N X D P O D L K Z S T F
Y A Q B A I G R G D Y N X R F M L L T C S O G
T A C R J B I A B R Y T O R T A S O I Z O U Q
D O I W R E S F L J T B L V Q B V J G N R K J
I N J V L Y U Q M E L R Y G H N H R H I S E C
G M T C Y H Z V U E Y S Q I J Z Q L E O Z D Q
I S U B O I H T M P Q M W M K E S O L V E E J
```

Chapter 5 Asking the Right Questions in Third Grade

```
K O L P I C Z G Q I X G H M M H V Y C A T G F
S Q O E A M K U O V M P N Z U C Y D B X Y Q J
A L A N J M N V J F U E M I Z O C R T H L A L
N Z Q V I L C P X R M C Y Y R U L J N L K F V
S Z I V G O U P K C A N V W O T E Z X Z Z B D
N Y J Z D E D Q N I S D Q S U D K W S K W I Z
P S P E C I F I C Y C F A T D G E K N B E R A
C K B G J P Q C T P L A R K Y P J S O X Q O E
Z D N I P N M T I M I N G G X Z V G I W N P C
T S I V Y R V A G A X G E C Y O X K T Q I W Q
W M V Q R L V F D E S C Z U V Z A V S I A I E
B B W K Q S O T W M H N W X D G T A E M L Z C
P O M K O J T L H R H G O Q R V P O U P P G U
H X H G Q S T H E L M W X C U E O D Q O X H R
F M G O B M L E R K N X Z Y X Q I R V R E P I
O S H T S Z B F E H W T H X H T Q F T L F O
N K H X J N S P W X A W B L P O I E L A L G U
H K N T K N P Q J H K V P T M S V E O N W K S
S D T Y F P D O W P P S R O T Y A N L T N O F
B C A M O E V G Q Q X H F N M R C Q Y C A A I
G F Y P H M L S W S M R A F N T C Y M T M H J
N T B S W G B Z N B W I Y E J T X W V P L W C
X J K U K W S J Y X M S C M S I L W W Q S S H
```

Chapter 6 How to Be a Great Team Player in Small Groups

```
C R X O Z B J O H S T B S M A L L S S U X J P
I E Q C Z E B R H S O U K O U C O D U F O C
Y G G G X U M R P A I N G N K K F D K X E W G
A T T K B B K P S R V D Y E T Q G B P L K L N
L R A E R W J H P I A S J Z T S T F G M D V I
T E A M W O R K L N N U E N S H P G M J F M N
U O Q Q E J Y D A G K I Y G B E E U O E O P E
K V L H K M H U Y J W V B M A P E R O E D B T
R U A I M H E V E N N W L B J R R P U R K V S
F L R C H G L O R Q B N W S S D U Q M F G N I
Q Y P S N M T L W E P F Z Y G I A O V F K M L
B Z J S B Q K E T E P B J X X Z E U C Z D D N
S A E D I F C A R N K O F K L W Y F C N I M M
B R Q Z X R M Y N M Q K J U S U N N C O E A T
I P T C X M E R G E Q D E H X F S U N G E C D
Z O D Q A B D M D J P K W H N A L N Z T X W V
Y P L E V V H R W C C R P S X E G F G H L G P
G R T J J O D N E P B S S Z O T X Y V Z M R W
H G F Q W P V M Y M X S K S P G N O I N I P O
S D H C F I T S A U O A E S I D X W Z N C X H
K A Q X L C I O L F X T J P D R Q O J S Z D P
Z F Q L D H I G E A D F O C F L R Q C J C X J
J Z J H T G E Y Q N Z H D B V W C O W G S K D
```

Chapter 7 How to Succeed in Studying Third Grade History

```
Q F H S U W R S E W R I T E G C H E X D J U H
C K Z C O V X U V W C S L S H A S Q P R T V A
W D Q L K N V Z S Q T W D X C U Z R F J X O U
F J P W E K V U T J Z L G X N H K T Z H D N S
Q X M Q X K I K N S T N B Y S V H P O U C U A
M O X M Q O K B M S K Z U Z F U Q X Q N W F N
L K J H I S T O R Y Y H A L T V O Q Y N H M G
I L G Z K E Q Z C S D X Y R Y U V I T W V T G
K E C H F I U W I O U L B O Z I X B R B F E X
P Z M A G V Q R E N T R A P Z Q U R W U B X M
A Q F Y T X J I G M S O T F X A W J F I C X E
K A G I Q U E S T I O N S R T G T E Y Y O P Q
Z T H Y Z A V E M M X I Q V X R W Q G R H X C
X Z P D Y E V N N J R R W X R S V N D S H W L
N D M N Y R O T S I P F V W T S L A U S I V U
C G C L F F Y V O K L Z E U N G S G A X I Z Q
C V M R E A L L I F E E D J K N X R S N X Z R
Z L D X I H U G N B H Y M O L M S I E G Q F I
V U E U D R D H O W I A R I O J C M M D W A K
H X T M J Y H C V N G M W O T S D F A E A C L
C U Z T K I E T G E U G N N Q B B U G A Y T K
H P V N N C Q P W V W S M W F T I R S V Q S J
I B Q R L Q C H G P L K S Z A M F Z X Z Z N B
```

134

Chapter 8 How to Succeed in Studying Third Grade Math

```
H B T A V D Y H J E R D U K H H A D I U F R G
T G K P R A C T I C E M N O F Z G M L E G N B
V L L Z M G F K E R N K S W Z B P Z X O I Z X
O V A I F U M E U E I O W P R M A Q J V D C O
G Z D H P X Y Z F B G S Z D E R M I L I E Z G
Q D O S S X I G O M G H V G W T O Z M D K D
S Q E U S M L A I E W H C Y X B S J P S W R B
B B P T L R Z O M K I A L H P R L Q H V V M
I L E J E W P P Q E L U O X T D S G O T E Z E
Q C T F V C N W E R W B I U L E P L D Y Y X W
K I Z N Y S T U N P N M F S Z C B L H Z D F C
M Q R J U X I I X L O L J Z F W S A N X T T X
I S Z N Y S Y R V B A R F X N X W M S S Q Z L
M A T H V R K B R E L L S A I O V S P K K T P
E C J U X B F N A Y Q U E S T I O N S J H K O
L L I K C D F F M K C C F L Y T P S P V Q L C
O F Z P J T U M G G D A K Y S T T T Z O P X S
I O K Z M L R S K C I R T S D O R Z M G S W D
Y N B O U B X O R T S P T Y S D S K A A E D O
A I K D V P K N H F L P Q M W N O R C P O X E
S S X X U F F T P S P L T S Y H X T I E L C F
C X M M V Q I O E N W I S G L C J F R H H O N
T O A H Y T G S Z M K W L K L A B Q H G A C Z
```

Chapter 9 How to Become a Reading Rockstar in Third Grade

```
K B B U L L C X B Y Y J U K L T Q F H T M I
N O T Y N Z E D E Y N O B Z H Q E R S W M M A
O I H S Z U J D B B P S B S T R A T E G I E S
J O X O O M F S E R I P Y O X Z X D U O L A Y
P U Q T V O V T A P M Y O Z Z C R D W S N X R
V O C X F V H C E M S J I D O Z U Q K E O J N
Q U X A Q R T S Y I R R R N C G R T K D G V
O W N U O I A W R J D A V G S U N S H L B Z J
Q Z O T C U G E S O R E I R L W I E K O F F P
G U N E V N G B R M R K M P A L D I G S D A I
M J F L Q Q N F A S N L U V O O A M U I U N E
P O I Z O G S D A W Y B A E G V E R C V I E H
A B C P K Q G T K G F G B Y A X R I N B Z O T
M C T K K V I P D H J G N O I T A N I G A M I
X Q I W M O E V E R Y D A Y Z F N D Z K T Q A
N L O J N P D M F D Q A U W L H L X O D K E T
G I N P K M X R U Q I H E C A U U H I C M O L
N F T B I U J S B O Z G T O F K U S F F F Z
C A W Z D U A B B X H S C O T T K M A W T D T
E X J R L O T U T O J W T B P O H H P V Z Y Q
V V R B R S M G P Z W A J O O S E G H D X C U
J J C C Q D B J G Z T N Z B D S E L N S H X Y
G H O Z G U E A Y Q K L G C E X O R X H R F W
```

136

Chapter 10 How to Crush It in Third Grade P.E.

Chapter 11 How to Be a Science Superstar in Third Grade

```
F M K D Y T D W W D T K X J T Y W C B P I W T
V H Y Q O V O R F W F T S F V N R S R P P J S
M W A H H Z E T S E Y S K B T C Y C L I B E R
Y P M V A K J G U O A N D F Z X N I I O L O O
R I V F W U J A U W U O M I N C U R V G P L A
V N Y C U D Z Q A Z R I K S D J O G G Y H T L
G U Q F T J P J V A C T C P Z G O O Q P V N S
N H W U W X X D Q F E S W W B L G X S R E P I
R A T S R E P U S T D E E D O X W F Q R Q U K
V E Q V E N Z V J E M U J N H M D R N S Y C A
Z C U R I O S I T Y N O H P L J R F F Q R W R
E X P E R I M E N T S C N U P F G C L K K P M
A W B C I Z S R S A E F G C B W H A N D S O N
F C C B I M P T O T G A E K Z G Q V U D F B M
S M H O H L O X O Q O R I S K R T X O R E W S
U P J U Q L V W B N P J O T L K Z J D T A W E
S M W P A M V W L H W H U W X V C E Y T P W P
E L V A J D H A Y T N G Z S T V X R C D M P A
N N I S W G N L F P R C R J A F R H W W S R S
S X C V B R K R D O Q J R B W S W D P X X X T
E T G Y U I Z B U C G I D Y C Y R S B L C Z N
S N O O Z Y Q P L V H F C G F P E C N E I C S
L I J M V I T D X B N S V T B Q C C D P A Q T
```

Chapter 12 How to Rock Third Grade Writing

```
R D R T G P X A W W S D G V O R T R C J O T I
I O I M A G I N A T I O N G S L G T O P Z B L
S K A P A S C D C Z R R F U S V O N E T S S W
G A F N P D K K N U A X M P Q B Z I K C C L
Z C K D Z R W X G E A V N M X W T Q Q V S X I
C U V G R O C X P N L Z Y S R N Q Y C A O V A
I G G I U W N P C I L I I S I N M M L J E K Q
A X U F S E N T E N C E S C F T B G M C F D S
C P K P K U K Z U P P Q N K W Y I J G I M P I
J Q B N I T Y P V K Z C G Z T B F O W X O Q D
W N G D R R A L Y N X S S N Z I I B N P D V J
U N Y S B Q P Z E R A H S U I H W D U O M Y F
F I H D I Z I Q T R C L O H H T D G T I D E R
K C A B D E E F Q B Q A P J L R I X Y B V O G
P H M A E I W H A S X C O S X A R E I I V K
I L X V T P E R S U A S I V E J F P W L Z W M
N Q C V A U K Z P Q V R Q U Q H E L E A M J M
U Q S E I E O H X E V O M U H Q P O G R V P S
M C P L L R I D A F E J M Q Q E D J T G T R Q
F Y W R S G N W W X I F N L P R A C T I C E P
Y N K S A T W A Z L A I Q F Z O X Q L T A C T
A S G B H W C D J Z W B K P V A E B C H F J B
K X J N Z X N X D T E S J G A B T U J N J T Q
```

Chapter 13 How to Conquer Third Grade Homework

```
U F R E O F C Q W W W E U B B B D P W W B D I
C K R O O B C A Z R T U P R E W A R D X U M O
P Q A T C H Y Z N A E Y D A E F A O E G Q E Z
E U N T V A C I N D Z E Y I L K W D E R F I N
D T A S S O V I B D F N K I B N A K D C Z S W
Y A E M Q J M T R H I N R G A I L M Q W X V U
L T U U E L U P V M F Z Z N Y A Z G H P J U M
C S L Y I R H A S W J A Q C O V Q A O H H S C
O U W E N O Z X S Y W Y G W J N J N R A V X O
P D S I S K K S B T F J R S N D J S F C W O H
Q U N Y P P Y W O I N Z F K E X E U R N L J L
G Y X I U Y X I R W M U A S A D J Q C J Z R K
Y V R C B N D S B Q P W K B I Y Q S B E G W F
T W H V R C O V B Q X Y K S B T D Q I C V M D
H G O X E L O X D F L E T C S F L O Z A Y H Y
Z K Q I A Z I K X F D R Y G U A C S U L N H M
E Y D X K B P L K J A A J F Y H H N B P C E R
E S K U S F T C Y C P L E H O F O B C O Q A O
K S G C Z A B V T L Q Z H O L S L M D S D M A
C L G W E F G I H O M E W O R K Z P U O I G Q
A Q Y V Z H Q W H W M Y S E L U D E H C S C J
H S C Q I N O F I X V H N O R G A N I Z E J F
K O K Y S F C O U W K Z G R O E R U Z L E W I
```

Chapter 14 How to Be an Exam-Ready Rockstar in Third Grade

```
P R S X D S W O S J K T M X B K G I C B N S R
K I X Y J Y C C P A X O U E A U A B F J N R M
A Z V Y B E Y Y Z Z H P C Y M Q K S J O L C A
E A C I E Q O P O R C S X N R O Q W I W N F S
K G Z A J T P S E F W T K E S W R T J K L C D
L E O E G D B N I P Q B Z Z P C S I O A B X B
V H N J K R T G R F S Z B P V E V I S A U X K
X W P F A R X A Z M U K X C U S B H C R R J P
Q J W E A Q C P Q Z B K A Q T N C D Y G P G A
E Q E P O T U H A Z L D S E R A K W F G G C N
C G L N I H F Z G R Q L H Z R L Q V S Q P S L
J V D C C G E P E N B U K D N B V L H Y R F X
R S E L K O R L H H A G S Z P V E G V M Y B R
M A X E J R Z A G W D H F T D E Z M S O V J E
X P H V Y V S N G T D H P H P Q K F Q E N E A
U W A I G P K J W V G V R W S G C W N H T J I
E W E T B V E M E M J S U E S T N A W V U O S
Z J Z O R B F K W Q Z E G K G W U H E X K G N
M Z E T N W Z P G P F A Q N H Q T D E T Q X B
P U Q F B Y K N Q S S U A E C B U H Y K X N T
L X C S M L X G R W Z P L E A T Y X W F R M Z
K G F R G J V A M P G V O U I M Q K O S Z V Z
Y K T B K J I Y L P T T O Y K N Q I Z I I N V
```

141

Other Books by Bobbie Anderson Jr.

- Fourth Grade Survival Guide
- Fifth Grade Survival Guide
- Sixth Grade Survival Guide

www.ingramcontent.com/pod-product-compliance
Lightning Source LLC
Chambersburg PA
CBHW051950290426
44110CB00015B/2181